Breaking Barriers

Breaking Barriers

IHC's First 50 Years

Julia Millen

PUBLISHED BY
IHC NEW ZEALAND (INC.)

First published in 1999 by IHC New Zealand (Inc.),
PO Box 4155, Wellington, New Zealand
and produced by
Bridget Williams Books Limited, PO Box 5482, Wellington

© IHC New Zealand (Inc.)

The publishers gratefully acknowledge permission to reproduce extracts from
To the Is-Land by Janet Frame, published by Random House (NZ) Ltd,
courtesy Curtis Brown (Aust) Pty Ltd, Sydney.
The author and publisher gratefully acknowledge the permission of individuals and
organisations for the reproduction of photographs in this book.

ISBN: 1 877 242 063

Typeset by Archetype
Internal design by Afineline
Cover design by Mission Hall Design Group
Printed by Astra Print, Wellington

Dedication

To people with intellectual disabilities and their families
– for uniqueness and courage

Contents

Acknowledgements

Dr C.P. Anyon, Dr D.M.G. Beasley, Dr R.T.M. Caseley, Marion Bruce, JB Munro, Lynne Renouf, Eileen Coulthard, Barbara Rocco, Jan Dowland, C.B. Waigth, Robin Allardyce, Allison Oosterman, A.P. Ranby, Barbara Adams, Dianne Bardsley, Tony Shaw, Jeff Sanders, Annette Lane, Michael Holdsworth, IHC Branch and office staff who researched/provided details for the appendices, Brio café for excellent coffee and ambience.

Special Acknowledgements

IHC's Library and Information Service Manager, Liz MacGibbon, and Advocate, Sue McKinnon. Liz has been a mine of information and unfailingly helpful responding to constant requests for assistance with source material. Sue McKinnon's appendices, including The Changing Language of Intellectual Disability (Appendix 1), add much value and interest to the book. She has meticulously researched and collated a wealth of detail.

Celia Dunlop
Communications and Marketing Manager, IHC

Julia Millen
Author

Foreword

IHC's history over 50 years tells a story of people from all walks of life passionately committed to, and united in, getting a better deal for people with an intellectual disability. Underpinning this commitment was, and is, an absolute belief that people with an intellectual disability must be valued and respected as unique individuals who have a right to live satisfying lives in the community. Today those values are expressed in IHC's Mission Statement and are the guiding principles of the organisation.

Fifty years ago dissatisfaction with the lack of services and the quality of those few that were provided was the impetus for parents to form the Intellectually Handicapped Children's Parents' Association (IHCPA).

Margaret and Harold Anyon travelled the length and breadth of New Zealand making contact with other parents and involving them in the battle for better facilities, better education and better opportunities for their sons and daughters.

Their demands were met by indifference at best, but more often by hostility, impatience, contempt and derision by those in authority. Undeterred, this group of parents persisted and gradually involved more and more parents, health professionals and community members in their cause.

Slowly and surely the tide turned. The rights of people with an intellectual disability to education, productive work, daytime activity and community-based accommodation became accepted by the authorities. Funding was made available to establish these services and IHC moved away from a sole advocacy focus to become a provider of services.

Today IHC is highly regarded nationally and internationally as a provider of support services to people with an intellectual disability and their families. It retains a strong advocacy focus and through a large network of people with an intellectual disability, their families, members and community supporters continues to ensure that gains, hard won over 50 years, are not eroded.

The story of IHC's rise from small beginnings to a large and vital national organisation is a celebration of the efforts of thousands of individuals – people with an intellectual disability, their families, members, staff and community supporters – working towards a common goal.

As we celebrate the first 50 years, thanks are due to all those who have been part of the journey until now. We can draw inspiration for the next 50 years from our founders who had the courage of their convictions and worked tirelessly to make them a reality.

Barbara Rocco
New Zealand President, IHC

Jan Dowland
Chief Executive, IHC

Notes

Changes in the Name of IHC

1949–62   Intellectually Handicapped Children's Parents' Association (Inc.)
1962–75   Intellectually Handicapped Children's Society (Inc.)
1975–94   New Zealand Society for the Intellectually Handicapped (Inc.)
1994–   IHC New Zealand (Inc.)

Intellectual Disability and Changes in Language: see Appendix 1.

1

Hidden Away and Desperate

In the Old Days ...

'Who is that funny person who lives with your grandmother?'

Surprised by the question from a school friend, Peter said, 'That's Elsie.'

Former Waikato branch president Peter Hanan remembers meeting Elsie at the age of six, in 1921. 'She enjoyed some of the fun and games with the four of us children. She had some authority over us but I used to wonder why she did not join the other grown-ups instead of staying with us.' Elsie was born in 1889 with Down's Syndrome. Her father died in 1892, leaving her mother with four girls under six. Elsie's mother, a woman of great courage and independence, became a school teacher and the family breadwinner while her own mother managed the family. Elsie received private teaching, learned to read and write and helped with the housework. Elsie and her mother grew old together, gradually becoming more and more isolated from community life. Elsie spent her last years copying the *Ancient and Modern Hymn Book* by hand, not always legibly.

Mavis, born 40 years later, remembers her early years.

> I went to Templeton when I was a baby in arms in 1928. My mother and father were fighting and I got hit on the head with a beer bottle and that's what

damaged my brain. They said I was a normal baby when I was born. I never went to school. They wanted me for the work because I was so good at it ... I learned to work when I was six years old. I had a little broom, a little hearth brush and shovel. They had you working four times a day. I used to help do the dishes and help look after the crippled kids in chairs and help the ones who couldn't help themselves ... Some nurses were cruel. They would hit us on the head with a wooden spoon ...

Another child born in the same era was luckier. Alice's first baby was born paralysed down the left side, spastic with an intellectual disability. Abandoned by medical professionals and with a husband who was supportive but very busy with his business, Alice had to cope with Ben alone. As was usual at that time, the education system refused to enrol Ben at school. Alice, undaunted and determined to do her best for her son, devised for him a caring and educational programme. She paid for private lessons with a tutor and Ben walked with his school bag to his teacher's home each day. Alice also sent her son to lessons in elocution and speech training. Meanwhile he learned to shop, write, read and knit. He and his mother went to the pictures, cowboy and Indian matinees: 'We both loved it,' Alice recalled.

When Alice was in her seventies she had a health breakdown. Ben, then aged 40, moved into a hospital but went home for weekends. At 67 Ben could still read all the family greeting cards and messages, sort out his favourite music and assemble the games he had always enjoyed.

Alice was an exception in many ways. She had a positive attitude, strength of character to fight for her son's rights and the means to bring up her disabled child in an enlightened manner. But even for her it was far from easy: she was alone in her stand – against public opinion, against expert advice. It was a life-long commitment: as a widow in her nineties, Alice continued to plan with methodical care for Ben's regular home visits.

New Zealand families with a child with a disability and limited resources faced huge difficulties in the early part of this century. In her autobiography *To the Island* writer Janet Frame tells of what happened to her own family living in Oamaru in the early 1930s.

Our lives were changed suddenly. Our brother had epilepsy, the doctor said, prescribing large doses of bromide, which, combined with Bruddie's now frequent attacks, or fits as everyone called them, only increased his confusion and fear until each day at home there were episodes of violent rage when he attacked us or threw whatever was at hand to throw.

Janet's brother Robert, born in 1922, had been a bright little boy until at the age of eight he began to exhibit these perplexing symptoms.

> Bruddie became stupefied by drugs and fits; he was either half asleep, recovering, crying from the last fit or in a rage of confusion that no one could understand or help. He still went to school where some of the bigger boys began to bully him, while we girls, perhaps prompted by the same feeling of fear, tried to avoid him ... Mother, resisting fiercely the advice of the doctor to put Bruddie in an institution, nursed him while we girls tried to survive on our own with the occasional help of Dad.

The Frame parents searched desperately for the cause of their little boy's problems, and despite having very little money, tried every conceivable treatment in their quest for a cure. Mrs Frame hoped that their son would 'grow out of it', while her husband believed that he could 'stop his fits if he wanted to'. Meanwhile the boy had to give up school.

> He educated himself with books that I brought home from the library and from the many books, originally from the library but now marked cancelled, that he found in the town rubbish dump ... There was little hope of a job for him, for when he did find one, someone would disclose that he had epilepsy and he'd be dismissed. 'They found out about me, Mum,' he'd say bitterly.

The ongoing costs of his medical treatment, both conventional and alternative, were far beyond the means of a Railways employee and the bills piled up. Mr Frame kept his creditors at bay with an occasional peace offering: a trout, some whitebait or a crayfish.

The first New Zealand act of Parliament that differentiated the mentally disabled from the mentally ill was the Mental Defectives Act of 1911, which replaced the Lunacy Act (1907). The new act clarified for official purposes what was meant by the term 'mental defective' by creating seven classes:

1. Persons of unsound mind.
2. Persons mentally infirm.
3. 'Idiots' – persons so deficient in mind from birth or from an early age that they are unable to guard themselves against common physical dangers and therefore require the oversight, care, or control required to be exercised in the case of young children.
4. 'Imbeciles' – persons who though capable of guarding themselves against common physical dangers are incapable or, if of school age, will

presumably when older be incapable of earning a living by reason of mental deficiency existing from birth or from an early age.

5. 'Feeble-minded' – persons who may be capable of earning a living under favourable circumstances but are incapable from mental deficiency existing from birth or from an early age of competing on equal terms with their normal fellows or of managing themselves and their affairs with ordinary prudence.

6. Epileptics.

7. Persons socially defective.

All those thus classified as mentally defective were, from the age of five years, to live in mental hospitals, with segregation of the sexes, under the responsibility of the Director General of Mental Defectives. Although the act made neglect or ill-treatment of such people an indictable offence, it paid minimal attention to their rights. The focus of the act was the plight of parents and guardians, and 'the public interest'. In the view of the medical establishment, whether they were 'sick' or developmentally delayed, 'mentally defective' people could not be treated by accepted medical methods, had no expectation of recovery from their condition and required only maintenance and rehabilitation.

The 1920s also saw medical experts emphasising eugenics issues, specifically fears that the mentally deficient or defective would breed and in so doing weaken the race. This led in part to the 1924 Committee of Inquiry into Mental Defectives and Sexual Offenders.

Anecdotal evidence from professionals in the fields of paediatrics and neo-natal care suggests that up until the 1930s and 1940s the family doctor usually discouraged the mother from even seeing the baby or taking it home from hospital if it had a disability. If a parent kept the child at home, few or no services were provided to help the mother or family. It was felt that the provision of community or home aid services would only encourage families to keep such children at home and the professional workers at the time felt an obligation to the family and the community to curb any such inclination. They even discouraged parents from maintaining contact with the child if it were placed in a state home. Such involvement was thought to create stress in other members of the family and promote health breakdown within the family.

Institutional Care

Official attitudes hardened: people with an intellectual disability had practically no potential, and no rights; little could be done except to house and feed them until death, in large institutions well away from the community. But mental hospitals and institutions, under the responsibility of the Department of Health, were designed for the treatment of the mentally ill and were ill-equipped to take those classed as mentally defective. Templeton Farm and Training School (near Christchurch) was established in 1929 but there was no equivalent institution in the North Island until Levin Farm in 1945.

But even in the officially termed 'mental deficiency institutions' conditions were appalling. Mavis describes her life at Templeton.

> We were in a big dormitory. There were 106 in the dormitory and they only had four windows, just that much open so you couldn't climb out. There were separate villas for the boys ... I didn't have any clothes of my own, not even underclothes. I didn't have anything of my own. I would wear the ward stuff, the stuff from the store. Because I came as a baby in arms I didn't have any of that ... Once someone else broke some windows. I was only 10 years old and I got the blame for this other girl. I was locked in a room with three locks on the door and just that much fresh air through the shutters. They didn't even let me out to go to the toilet. I fainted on them.

Facilities were also inadequate: a particular problem was that there was no separation of children from adults. Parents also recall that their children on weekend leave often arrived home with health problems that had been neglected; and clothing was frequently found to be missing, laundered incorrectly or mixed with that of other residents, causing parents constant extra expense in replacements. It seemed to them that the physical comfort of the 'mentally deficient' was considered less important than that of the mentally ill.

The late 1930s brought new hope: for relief of suffering and for social justice. Janet Frame remembers vividly the election of the first Labour government with its promise of social security, free medical treatment and free hospital treatment for all. By that time the Frame family's debts for medical treatment for her brother's epilepsy were so enormous her parents had given up all hope of paying them. 'When the Social Security Act was finally passed, Dad, in a spontaneous dance of delight in which the family joined, removed the bills from behind the clock and, taking the poker from its hook by the stove, lifted the cover and thrust all the bills into the fire.'

The passage of this legislation in 1938, however, also heightened the difference between the departments of Health and Education. While children in the care of the Mental Hygiene Division of the Department of Health remained in institutions, excluded from any benefits of the welfare state, the Department of Education had some time earlier begun special classes to educate some slow learners who stayed at home with their families. The New Zealand Education Act of 1877 provided for all children including the 'feeble-minded' to have access to free, secular education, but for the latter it was not compulsory. The Child Welfare Division of the Department of Education had set up two special residential schools. Otekaike, near Oamaru in north Otago (later known as Campbell Park School) was opened by the department in 1908 as a residential school for 'feeble-minded' boys. Salisbury School for 'feeble-minded' girls was opened in Richmond (near Nelson) in 1916. Stoke Farm was established in 1922. It was noted also that many of the 'feeble-minded' were attending ordinary schools, but administrators were less happy to note the presence of older children in the infant classes and saw the need, ideally, for special classes.

In 1944, with the end of the war in sight, the air force moved out of its base in Horowhenua and the Department of Health took over the facilities to establish what was known as Levin Farm. Mavis, by then aged 18, was moved there from Templeton along with 20 others.

> The place was dirty. The kids had cradle cap in their heads. I had it too. You have sores all over your body, little kiddies too. One [nursing] sister came and said: 'What have the kids got in their hair?' 'Nits', I said. 'Well the staff can't be looking after them properly,' she said. She used to trust me to lock the stores. She got me good clothes from the store, she picked the best out for me.

At Levin, as at Templeton, Mavis spent most of her time working. 'They used to like me because I did it properly. I used to be fussy about that. I worked in the laundry too, for nine years until I fell on the stove getting my dinner ... I fainted and fell on the electric stove and spent a long time in hospital in Palmerston North with skin grafts.' In contrast with her day-to-day life at Levin Farm the hospital seemed to Mavis like paradise. 'That hospital was lovely. They were friendly. They wanted to keep me there to give me schooling, but Levin wouldn't hear of it.'

Others were also disillusioned about Levin Farm. Wrote one parent: 'Levin Farm is not a farm. The farm has been leased and the title is misleading. Neither

is it a school. There are no departmental teachers educating the children.' A
father described the experiences of his son:

> My child was admitted to Levin at six years of age and on the understanding
> that occupational therapy would be available. At Levin Farm he was two years
> without any occupational therapy. In his third year he had a short time with
> the one and only therapist who relinquished him because:
> 1. He needed individual attention to help him concentrate and she could not
>   spare the time, though he was capable of doing the work. This was unavoid-
>   able owing to staff shortages.
> 2. He could not be sent unattended to the lavatory in the block where he
>   lived. There was no lavatory at the occupational room and there was only
>   one therapist present who could not leave the other children unattended.
> He went to Levin a bright, happy, normal-looking child. There he became
> listless and dull through absolutely no occupation, not even walks in the
> grounds.

Another report confirms his view: 'In June 1950, children at Levin Farm
appeared dispirited and forlorn. They had no outside toys and enquiry about
toys brought the answer, "They break them."'

The end of the war brought peace and hopes for a better world. Postwar
reforms in New Zealand, as in other western democracies, emphasised human
rights issues. People who had experienced the deprivations and social injustices
of the 1930s Depression years and witnessed the atrocities of World War II
understood the need for safeguards to prevent the possibility of recurrence.
They wanted a fairer society so that the sacrifices of the war years would not
have been in vain. Although there was still a great deal of stigma attached to
people with an intellectual disability and their parents, for the first time it was
beginning to be argued that people with learning difficulties should receive
the rights accorded other members of society.

Pioneering Efforts in Auckland, Wellington and Dunedin

On 23 February 1933 parents and citizens of Auckland met at Myers Park
Special School with the idea of forming an After-Care Association and an
occupational centre for their 'backward' children. As happened elsewhere, a
committee was formed but parent representatives were excluded. The following

year, on 30 August, the Auckland After-Care Association was disbanded and a new organisation formed, the Institute for the Care of Backward Children. Once again, parents had little say. Later that same year a class was set up at Newton East School (later known as Sunnydene) under the control of the Auckland Education Board. Within a year there were 26 pupils, aged between seven and 18 years, on the roll.

In 1936 a Wellington couple, Margaret and Harold S. (Hal) Anyon, received devastating news. A doctor told them that their youngest child, then only 10 months old, would never go to school and that Margaret herself 'deserved some-thing better'. Keith had been born with Down's Syndrome. While most parents in their situation would have placed such a child in an institution, this option was not considered by the Anyons. From the beginning Margaret was deter-mined that something could and would be done for her youngest child.

Their elder son, Dr Peter Anyon, recalls that Margaret Anyon was tireless in her efforts, taking Keith to see one doctor after another, trying any and every possible treatment. One of many avenues tried was seawater treatment. Peter remembers a family summer holiday at Raumati Beach soon after Keith was born. One of his twice-daily chores was to collect buckets of seawater and carry them up the sandhill to the bach where they were staying. There his mother heated the water in a cut-down kerosene tin on the stove for Keith's 'special baths'. It was only the beginning of the Anyon family's life-long commitment to Keith.

After two years the same doctor who had at first offered little hope told the Anyons that Keith 'would go a long way'. But it was Dr Charles Burns, whose work was of later significance to the IHC, who offered the Anyons the most encouragement. His positive attitude was in total contrast to that of many in the medical profession at the time. When he told the Anyons their son 'should be educable in a special class', it was a turning point for Margaret Anyon.

In the course of her research into her son's condition she had read an article in the New Zealand Education Gazette (1943) entitled 'Finding the Backward Child'. It told her that educational support was available in the form of postal lessons from the New Zealand Correspondence School. The Anyons duly enrolled Keith in the Correspondence School, which enabled him to do school work at home with supervision from his mother. There was also provision for disabled children to have short stays at health camps. Occupational centres were by now functioning in a few areas but not Wellington. When the Anyons tried to enrol their son in a special class Keith was refused admission by the supervisor. The day-care centre run by the After-Care Association agreed to take Keith, but Margaret was told it catered mainly for older children who did not in any case receive any education there. She enrolled him anyway: at least he would have companionship.

She discovered that the After-Care Association had no children's play equipment of any kind, nor furnishings suitable for small children. The volunteers who ran the centre were in the main 'do-gooders' with no educational training; all they did was keep those in their care occupied and happy. 'Children sat for an hour at a time at handwork and then after having afternoon tea, enjoyed an hour of games and music.'

Margaret Anyon later wrote:

> During 1944 and 1945 other parents of younger children as well as myself asked [the After-Care committee] for educational help. We were told that 'the Board would not approve and that the Education Board knew that the After-Care Association was doing everything necessary for the children, also that there were not enough children for a centre.

The Anyons rapidly became activists. Despite the fact that, as in Auckland, parents had not previously been accepted as members of the executive committee, Margaret Anyon became honorary secretary of the After-Care Association. Her experience prior to her marriage as secretary to a cabinet minister meant she was well qualified. One of the many things Margaret discovered was that the After-Care Association had some months earlier refused the offer of a teacher from the Education Department. Neither she nor any of the other parents who had been seeking such help had been told of this offer.

Margaret Anyon then visited Dunedin to look at a training school being run by a committee of representatives of the YWCA, Kindergarten Association, representatives of various school old girls' associations and the Otago branch of the National Council of Women, under the aegis of the Department of Education. At the centre, in Moray Place, Margaret Anyon found children of a similar ability to her son Keith receiving educational help. She later wrote in praise of the way the centre was managed: 'A good meal prepared by a competent cook was well served and children assisted with the simpler parts of washing up and cleaning down benches.' She also visited a hostel at Abbotsford for children with an intellectual disability run by the Otago Education Board; this had opened in 1946.

Back in Wellington she put forward a motion to the After-Care Committee that it urge the Education Board to establish a similar type of school in the capital. For some reason this motion was never voted on and not long after, Margaret Anyon resigned as secretary of After-Care and withdrew Keith from the centre, writing: 'I feel I can do more to help him and other little ones if freed from my present duties.'

As he was growing up Keith received the full attention of his parents and was allowed considerable freedom of movement. Too much freedom, according to Peter, who remembers spending hours riding his bike around the streets near their home looking for his young brother.

Meanwhile Margaret Anyon continued her efforts to obtain further education for Keith. By the late 1940s Peter Anyon was studying medicine at Otago University. At that time, Margaret Anyon had a cousin who was a retired teacher living in Invercargill and she arranged for Keith to live with this cousin and receive special coaching. Peter remembers that when he returned to university after the long vacation he was charged with the task of delivering his young brother first to Invercargill. It was a long journey involving an overnight trip on the ferry, and an all-day train journey. At the end of the term Peter would go back to Invercargill to collect his younger brother and escort him by train and ferry back home to Wellington. He sometimes wondered if the effort was worth while, as any benefit to Keith seemed short lived, but the Anyon parents were pleased with Keith's progress. His diction had improved and he could do simple arithmetic. It reinforced their view on the benefits of education.

The Anyons launched a campaign for an occupational centre in Wellington. Margaret approached James Caughley, Supervisor of Psychological Services, and wrote many letters to the Wellington Education Board, the Department of Education and the Minister of Education. She was in her element: she had the commitment and was uniquely qualified for the task in hand.

On 12 August 1948 the Anyons received welcome news from Education Minister T.H. (later Sir Terence) McCombs: the Wellington Education Board was endeavouring to establish a centre. Two months later the board wrote that it was looking for a site for the proposed centre. But it was not until the following July that the board informed Mrs Anyon that a government property in Oriental Bay had become available. However, work needed to be done and the centre would not be completed until the end of October 1949. In the meantime Margaret Anyon had written to the Minister requesting greater parent representation on the committees running occupational centres. She received confirmation that the administrative committee of the proposed new centre would have two parent representatives.

Keith Anyon was now 14. For seven years his parents had been fighting for his right to be educated. They now started on a new tack. The Anyons asked the Wellington Education Board to provide the names of parents of prospective pupils of the new centre. They received a list of 16 names. October came but no centre had appeared. It was time for action.

2

The Anyons Take Action

The Anyons in Action

Parents and guardians of backward children in the Wellington district are invited to attend a meeting in the BMA Rooms, The Terrace, tomorrow at 8.00pm. The purpose of the meeting will be to consider the formation of a parents' association which will link with other associations in other centres. The Occupational Centre to be opened shortly at Oriental Bay by the Education Board will also be discussed. The meeting has been convened by a group of parents. (*Evening Post*, 24 October 1949)

At the appointed hour 22 parents, including the Anyons, arrived at this inaugural meeting. Six families were represented by both parents, and there were another eight mothers and two fathers present. Margaret Anyon later noted that between them these parents had three children in special classes, one child in Levin Farm, eight children with Down's Syndrome, two children with cerebral palsy, one child with brain damage and one other child (condition unspecified).

The meeting appointed an interim committee: Hal Anyon (chairman), Margaret Anyon (secretary-treasurer), Olive Grenfell and C. Outhwaite (committee). These four were given the task of formulating a policy and drawing up a constitution for the proposed association. The parents at the meeting also expressed indignation at the delays in completion of the Oriental Bay occupational centre.

The Anyons worked well as a team; their skills were different but complementary. Hal Anyon was a building contractor, a practical man of action with an outgoing personality. There are numerous references in the early literature to Hal Anyon's work urging for the building of suitable amenities, approaching government agencies, constantly making reports in the media.

Margaret Anyon was in many ways the driving force behind the campaign. A woman of considerable intellect, she was former dux of Southland Girls' High School, with a reserved and undemonstrative personality and great organisational ability. She typed and distributed letters, minutes and other documents and arranged for telegrams to be sent to Prime Minister Peter Fraser and T.H. McCombs, the Education Minister protesting at the 'lack of expenditure on the education of handicapped children'. Although reporters had been barred from the inaugural meeting Mrs Anyon sent out press releases. The *Southern Cross* reported:

> The secretary said yesterday it was necessary to awaken the country's responsibility to a class of children at present ignored by society, but who could with proper training be adjusted to good citizenship. The most urgent requirement stressed at the meeting was the need for the establishment of educational facilities.

Less than a month later, on 23 November, a second meeting, held this time at the NZEI Rooms in Willis Street, was attended by 50 parents: the campaign set in motion by the Anyons was starting to snowball. This meeting officially set up the Intellectually Handicapped Children's Parents' Association as an incorporated society and elected a New Zealand committee: Hal Anyon (president), Olive Grenfell (vice-president), Margaret Anyon (honorary secretary) and Tom Brydone (honorary treasurer). Committee members were Mrs R. Morris, and Messrs A.C. Buckley, R. Graves and C. Outhwaite.

Notable was the official name of the new association. Parents had looked for a non-pejorative term to describe children who at that time were called mentally deficient, retarded, feeble-minded or backward. James Caughley, Supervisor of Psychological Services, was sympathetic to the parents' cause, and although not able to attend the meeting, had suggested the term 'intellectually handicapped'. This term adopted by the society has remained unique to New Zealand and was originally defined to include '... any child whose mental or educational development is hindered or prevented by reason of mental or physical defect and shall be deemed to extend to and include adult persons who have suffered from such defect in childhood and continue so to suffer'.

The main goal of the association was to be a voice and a support for those intimately connected with people with an intellectual handicap. The interim committee had drawn up a draft constitution which was endorsed by the meeting. Tom Brydone, treasurer of the new association, a lawyer then working with the Justice Department in Wellington and the parent of a child with an intellectual disability, helped write the rules and regulations. The Anyons, who had played a large part in drawing up the constitution, were determined that only parents or legal guardians should become members with a right to vote and hold office; free from interference from non-parents – so-called professionals, experts and officials. Non-carers could be 'associate members' but could not vote or hold office. The objects of the association numbered 11 in all, the principal one being: 'To promote the physical, educational, economic and social welfare of intellectually handicapped children.' The constitution included rules and regulations about how the association was to be run, rules for the formation and running of branches and for a national executive body.

It was trail-blazing work, as Margaret Anyon later wrote:

> It must be remembered that we had no precedents for our claim, no literature, no knowledge of other countries' work, no trained people, no [government] department and practically no political anxiety to assist, no money, no relief in our homes. We had no occupation centres, no short-stay homes, and institutions as they were then were deplorable from our point of view and without accommodation for any increased demand. We had to explain at every turn what we meant by an intellectually handicapped child.

From this point the founders did not sit at home waiting for something to happen; they went out to meet the world. Rae Gale remembers the early days of the IHC in Auckland.

> In 1949 my late husband Phil Woods and I were living at Brown's Bay on Auckland's North Shore with our eight-year-old son Philip. We were just going through a period of adjustment having learned that he was microcephalic and was unable to attend normal school ... As young parents we didn't know any other family anywhere who had a handicapped child. It was a frightening situation.

So it was with mounting excitement that the Woods saw a newspaper report of the formation in Wellington of the Intellectually Handicapped Children's Parents' Association. The article said the association's President, Hal Anyon, and a group of supporting parents, were to travel throughout New Zealand forming branches. Rae and her husband went into the city on the night of the Auckland meeting. 'We were surprised and delighted to see a crowd of some 60 people obviously representative of a wide section of society. This one factor did much to lift our spirits, but greater things were to follow.' Hal Anyon had a captive audience, and to the people in the hall that night his words were like gold. He and Margaret Anyon and other Wellington parents, including Tom Brydone, described their prolonged battle with government departments and bureaucracy for a better deal for the handicapped.

Other parents later described that first meeting as a turning point. The newly formed Auckland branch elected Ted Woolley the first president, and he was succeeded the following year by Stanley Luker. Rae recalls that communication between the Auckland committee and the members was good and they were kept well informed about meetings. In 1951 Rae was elected on to the executive of the Auckland branch and the New Zealand Committee.

Public Opposition

One of the first acts of the newly incorporated IHCPA in Wellington was to send a telegram to the Minister of Education protesting at the delay in readying the Oriental Bay site and seeking an assurance that the centre would soon be opened. But the general election that month saw the Labour government ousted by National and the association had to wait for the new Minister of Education, R.M. Algie, to consider the matter.

Meanwhile, residents of Oriental Bay had become aware of the proposals for a centre and many were not happy about it. A group of residents started a petition in opposition. The *Dominion* newspaper reported in January 1950: '... the petition says that it is undesirable that such an institution should be established in a closely built up city residential area and that in the interests of the children a centre should be set up in some rural or sparsely populated area.' The petitioners claimed that the children would be in danger because of the traffic on the road at the front of the property. It was the beginning of what became a prolonged and widespread public debate that highlighted many of the prejudices prevalent at the time.

N.R. Seddon, chairman of the Wellington Education Board, replied to the petitioners in support of the centre: '... suggestions that the children be transferred to a rural area showed a lack of knowledge of the facts. The institution was to be a day school with about 30 children, drawn from a wide area, so a central location was necessary so transport could be arranged.' A 'Resident' then wrote to the *Dominion* requesting consideration in respect of the 'deterioration of our locality'. At last the petitioners' real concerns were in the open. They cared less about the children than about their property values. Opinion among the populus at large became sharply divided. One correspondent wrote criticising the petitioners:

> It would be bad enough if these people came right out into the open and said they didn't want a handful of backward children around the place, even for a few hours a day. That they should do their sniping from behind the camouflage of concern for the children stamps this perfidious petition as utterly mean and unworthy of Wellington.

The IHCPA met on 20 February 1950 to discuss the situation and sent a letter to the Prime Minister seeking his assurance that the occupational centre would proceed. Sid Holland replied: 'A final decision is delayed owing to the illness of the Minister of Education. I can do no more at the moment.' It seemed that the new government was stalling.

The blow fell a month later. The government announced that the site had been rejected as too costly to upgrade. The Education Board would be instructed to look for an alternative site, suitable for a purpose-built school. Privately IHCPA members felt that the National government had bowed to prejudice and pressure from the good citizens of Oriental Bay.

Looking for a Home

The association latched on to the positive news:

> To know that the great need for proper facilities in Wellington has been recognised and that suitable provision will be made gives great hope to parents of younger children. A completely new building in suitable surroundings would of course be ideal but the numbers waiting for help are so high that

the delay again involved further increases the distress already evident. If a property can be obtained ... with a building that can be used temporarily and with space available for future building the situation could be met at once. (*Evening Post*, 31 March 1950)

The IHCPA enlisted the support of several MPs to their cause. On 26 April the Leader of the Opposition, Peter Fraser, headed a deputation to the Minister of Education suggesting a temporary centre be established in the Basin Reserve pavilion. The Minister agreed.

On 23 May 1950 the parents brought their children to the pavilion. Disappointment awaited them. No preparations had been made to receive the children: the place was cold and not even clean. The toilets were up three flights of stairs and there was no toilet paper or soap. Margaret Anyon and other parents complained to the Minister of Education and the Minister of Children's Affairs, Mrs (later Dame) Hilda Ross, who visited the centre along with representatives from the Education Board. Mrs Ross in particular spoke out strongly about the inadequate conditions and as a result the place was cleaned and some of the other deficiencies, such as lack of heating, were rectified. With much of the equipment provided by the parents, within a few months this centre was catering for 24 children, making the most of what was available. Like many temporary measures, the Basin Reserve pavilion had to serve as a centre for much longer than planned.

Of major concern to parents was the teacher appointed by the Education Board. She taught only games and handcrafts and was opposed to 'academic' education that would put too much 'strain' on the children.

The search for a permanent occupational centre continued. In July 1950 parents rejected a site in Island Bay suggested by the board. It had already been deemed unsuitable for a school because it was low and damp, and the IHCPA was 'not going to accept what was considered unsuitable for normal children'. At this point Hal Anyon took matters into his own hands and wrote to the Minister of Education and the board suggesting three properties he had discovered were on the market. His preference was for a site in Coromandel Street, Newtown. The Leader of the Opposition (Peter Fraser), Minister of Health (J.T. Watts), Minister of Education (R.M. Algie) and Prime Minister (Sid Holland) were all involved in the ongoing debate. Finally in September 1950 the Wellington Education Board purchased the three-quarter-acre section in Coromandel Street suggested by Hal Anyon. Work went on to design a suitable building, prepare the grounds and make extra equipment.

The Wellington occupational centre moved out of the Basin Reserve pavilion to the Coromandel Street site in 1952 and was opened by the Minister of Education on 2 September with a roll of 18 children.

One of the children who attended the Coromandel Street Centre in the early years was the daughter of Eileen Coulthard. Trish, born with brain damage in 1941, was then aged 12 and her parents had been trying for some years to find appropriate schooling for her. Before she was admitted to the new centre Eileen had taken her daughter to a doctor for assessment.

'I'm afraid your daughter is retarded,' the doctor had said coldly.

Eileen Coulthard protested: 'But she's intelligent, she can do lots of things.'

'So can animals,' came the reply.

For Eileen it was a distressing start, but sending her daughter to the centre was in the end a positive experience. 'The children were picked up from home and taken by taxi five days a week. Although she gained no academic training there, Trish learned handcraft and other skills and enjoyed the social contact with other children.'

The Dominion Conference

Within weeks of the founding of the IHCPA the committee invited parents from all over New Zealand to attend a conference in Wellington with a view to forming branches in other centres.

The Dominion Conference was held in the Wellington Education Board rooms on 27 April 1950. In those days it was a considerable commitment in time as well as money to make the trip to Wellington, especially for South Islanders. Most parents who came were personally acquainted with the Anyons, who had at their own expense travelled up and down New Zealand looking for parents of handicapped children, finding them everywhere. At the conference were parents from Auckland (5), Christchurch (2), Dunedin (2), Nelson (1) and Invercargill (1). (Invercargill and Dunedin already had branches of the IHCPA.)

The Dominion Conference resolved to set up a New Zealand IHCPA Council, representing all the branches. This policymaking body would meet once or twice a year. Between council meetings ongoing business would be carried out by a New Zealand IHCPA Committee consisting of Wellington members plus representatives from other areas. They would try to form branches in other areas, particularly the main towns. In their areas, branches should work first for the establishment of occupational centres and also short-stay homes where children could be cared for while their parents were sick or on holiday. In the long term they should work for permanent small local homes for children whose parents could no longer look after them. The underlying philosophy set down at this time was to remain unchanged in essence throughout the next 50 years. Parents wanted three things: education, occupation and homes for their children.

Half a century later, founder members remember that IHCPA meetings were stormy affairs. Organisers and delegates felt under tremendous pressure to get something done for parents. Jean Clark, an early committee member whose second child, Campbell, was born in 1945 with brain damage and later developed epilepsy, remembered the early days of IHC meetings as lively, argumentative, idealistic and stormy. 'We'd be on our feet yelling at one another,' Rae Gale agrees. 'This was the period in our history where you got up on your feet and verbally battled for everything that you believed in. It was a time when cabinet ministers, officers of such departments as Health or Education faced conferences and met the arguments head on.'

The IHCPA's extraordinarily rapid growth provided graphic illustration that the needs of parents of handicapped children were not being met. They came from all walks of life. Most believed, or hoped, that their children's abilities and the quality of life for them and their families would increase with proper education.

In addition to those in Southland and Otago, new branches formed in Auckland, South Auckland (based in Hamilton), Christchurch, Wanganui and Hawke's Bay. Less than 18 months later the association had 10 branches and 600 members and was holding its first annual conference. Margaret Anyon wrote in January 1951:

> Since the inception of the IHCPA parents in towns outside of the four main cities have made determined efforts to provide their children with occupation and companionship. Until one of the centres was opened in Hastings in May 1951, there was no educational assistance or social training for children in towns of similar size ...

Because of the distances and expense of travel the New Zealand Council of the IHCPA often met only at the annual conference. This meant that the heavily Wellington-based New Zealand committee, in effect the management sub-group of the council, was left to co-ordinate the work of the branches and negotiate with the government. Many members from other districts resented this Wellington domination, but economic necessity made it inevitable. The first elected senior positions were held by the Wellington founder members.

President: Hal Anyon (Wellington)
Vice-president: Olive Grenfell (Wellington)
Hon. Treasurer: J.J. Doyle (Wellington)
Hon. Secretary: Margaret Anyon (Wellington)
The rest of the council consisted of Mrs B. Gordon (Auckland), A.H. Helleur (Napier), L. Ivil (New Plymouth) and R.W.S. Botting (Dunedin).

On 1–2 March 1951 two representatives from each branch plus the Wellington committee met for the first time as the New Zealand Committee. Out-of-town committee and council members either paid their own travel expenses or were paid for by their branches. One or two South Island representatives such as Stan Botting could not attend in 1951 because of the waterfront dispute. Botting later tried to save the branch money by timing his NZRFU council meetings to coincide with his IHCPA ones. From 1952 travel expenses were met by a capitation from all the branches.

In his inaugural presidential speech Hal Anyon outlined what he considered should be the association's goals:

1. Education for five- to 18-year-olds.
2. Occupation for those in the 18-plus age group in the style of 'trade training centres'.
3. So-called 'cottage homes' established to replace the large state institutions.

At the first full conference branches were able to report that Auckland and Dunedin already had occupational centres, and Auckland was also planning a hostel. Other branches were lobbying their local education boards for occupational centres. Several members noted the problem that although many parents were interested, some were reluctant to come forward and make it known that they had a child with an intellectual disability.

Margaret Anyon wrote about the association in the *New Zealand Child Welfare Workers' Bulletin*, 1951:

> The aim of the Association is to promote the social, economic, educational and physical welfare of the children by parent co-operation and interest ... [to] make direct contact with those responsible for establishment of hostels,

schools, occupational centres and homes and endeavour to encourage and use advances in psychological and medical research. Interest in the child will be maintained throughout childhood and adulthood and continued by the Association in the event of the death of parents or guardian.

Petitioning Parliament

At the Dominion Conference in April 1950 the Wellington committee had distributed a petition drawn up to present to Parliament: their target was 5000 signatures. Parents took petition forms back home to circulate in their own areas. The petition asked for Parliament to set up a special committee, including departmental and medical specialists and parents:

1. To enquire into and formulate proposals to remedy the anomalies which deny to the handicapped child the educational, health and social amenities enjoyed by the normal child.
2. To enquire into and formulate proposals to remedy the lack of suitable residential care for these children.
3. Generally to formulate proposals to stimulate research — medical, social and otherwise – so that a comprehensive scheme may be provided to meet the needs of all these children throughout their lives.

Although they fell somewhat short of their target of 5000, the petition with 3294 signatures was presented to the House of Representatives by J.R. Hanan MP on 2 August 1950 and IHCPA representatives gave evidence before a select committee of the House. The association asked Parliament to set up a Care of Children Committee to co-ordinate the needs of disabled children. Among its submissions were specifications of the kinds of educational facilities required, along with an outline of the need for free speech therapy, research into mental deficiency, and home aids for mothers. The parents also requested 'cottage homes' as alternatives to the existing mental hospitals and mental deficiency colonies.

The Mental Hygiene Division of the Department of Health gave evidence to the select committee which in many ways contradicted that of the association. 'It is generally accepted that any long-term residential provision for the mentally deficient is best done by means of the colony type of institution ... such as Templeton and Levin with accommodation for, say, five hundred to one thousand beds.' Their rationale was basically economic but also stemmed from concern to protect families from the burden of caring.

The select committee recommended that the IHCPA petition be referred for 'most favourable consideration'. In August the following year, 1951, Prime Minister Sid Holland announced the setting up of a Consultative Committee of Inquiry to:

> ... consider facilities provided for intellectually handicapped children between the ages of 4 and 18 and for those over 18 years of age, and to make such recommendations as it sees fit. The term 'intellectually handicapped children' is to be taken to mean children who are incapable of deriving instruction from special classes in public schools.

So far so good. But though pleased that the government had taken notice of its petition, the IHCPA was not at all satisfied with the composition of the committee:

> Dr R.S. Aitken, Vice-Chancellor, University of Otago
> Dr L.S. Davis, Director, Division of School Hygiene
> Dr G.M. Tothill, Deputy-director, Division of Mental Hygiene
> F.C. Lopdell, Chief Inspector, Primary Schools
> James C. Caughley, Supervisor, Psychological Services

Hal Anyon made a strong protest to the press. Not only were there no parent representatives on the committee, but there were no social workers and no women. Only after further requests from the IHCPA was a Miss Jean M. Robertson, a senior lecturer in social science at Victoria University College, added to the Consultative Committee.

Hal and Margaret Anyon were tireless, passionate – some said fanatical – in their efforts on behalf of parents. J.R. (later Sir John) Marshall became Minister of Health in 1951 and recounted his dealings with the Anyons in his memoirs.

> I had not been long in office when I was confronted by the President Mr Anyon and his wife, parents of a Down's Syndrome child and ardent campaigners for a better deal for handicapped children. They told me about their boy. I expressed my sympathy. They did not want sympathy – they loved their son. They were training him to do many things a normal child could do. They did not want him to go to a mental home as long as they were alive and able to care for him. They wanted more government interest and support for children with an intellectual disability and their parents in schooling and training, transport and employment and short stay homes ... The Anyons were

rather demanding and critical as people emotionally involved often are. It was not enough for me to say that the schools and health services were already doing a great deal to help ... they had a list of things to be done and their association was going to see that the Government did them. There were other parents, more gentle but just as dedicated who added to the pressure.

Anecdotes abound about the Anyons' dedication, and one in particular serves to illustrate Margaret Anyon's courage and single-mindedness. When the Minister she needed to see (R.M. Algie) continued to evade her by slipping out a back exit, she determined that he was going to listen to her, come what may. She blocked the entrance to his office early one morning (it was rumoured that she had slept in the foyer of Parliament) and caught him unawares.

The IHCPA settled down to prepare submissions to the Consultative Committee. One would be on behalf of the New Zealand Committee. A circular went to the branches, who would prepare their own submissions, outlining some of the points they should consider.

The Consultative Committee began hearing evidence in Auckland in February 1952, where it heard submissions from IHCPA branches in Northland, Auckland and South Auckland. It then travelled south throughout the country hearing submissions from IHCPA branches and inspecting facilities catering for people with an intellectual disability: mental hospitals, mental deficiency colonies, occupational centres and groups.

On 5 June 1952 Margaret Anyon and Mr Laurenson presented a 43-page submission on behalf of the New Zealand Committee that stated the problem quite unequivocally. 'The present State institutions are entirely inadequate to meet the needs of the children and to satisfy the desire of their parents for suitable homes.' With graphic illustration they testified that far from improving, children admitted to Levin and Templeton deteriorated physically and mentally. The submission outlined the kind of constructive work that would be possible for the children to undertake given appropriate teaching.

> They can make simple toys, baskets, weave, make seed boxes, grow seedlings, transplant them, bundle them up, pack kindling, soap, clothes-pegs etc. Responsible children can weigh unbreakables very accurately. Boys can be taught rough boot-mending. Girls can sew, do domestic tasks. Both can weave, knit and do handwork of variety.

An example given was of an unnamed child who had become acquainted with the local shoemaker and would sit in his shop and watch him at work. This child was in fact Keith Anyon. The boy, the submission continued, 'showed particular aptitude for use of the tools and [a] shoemaker recognised the anxiety to work and the reliability that was concealed beneath a deceptive exterior. Recently the shoemaker offered to teach the child to mend boots as soon as he left school ...' He also, under benevolent supervision, dealt with customers and handled small monetary exchanges. After a period of special coaching in Invercargill Keith was able to find employment and became well known to residents in the suburb of Khandallah, where the family lived, for his work at the shoemaker.

The submission criticised the Mental Hygiene Division and pressed for the provision of cottage homes. Asked to be more specific, the Wellington members of the New Zealand Committee met on 9 June and wrote a further submission on cottage homes. These would be villas containing a maximum of 25 children with a maximum of seven villas at each location. Each villa would have its own dining room, a separate bedroom for each child and an independent staff of four adults. The homes would provide occupational facilities for all ages, and would be near city centres in 16 districts.

Crude and Ill-Considered: The Aitken Report

The Report of the Consultative Committee, known as the Aitken Report, was released in February 1953. The committee's recommendations were summarised in 10 points. The main thrust was to endorse the concept of residential institutions and to encourage parents to place intellectually handicapped children in these institutions from about the age of five years.

The IHCPA New Zealand Committee bought many copies and distributed them to the branches with a list of comments. To say that the New Zealand Committee was disappointed with the Aitken Report would be a gross understatement. Use of the terms 'idiot', 'imbecile' and 'feeble-minded' were particularly discouraging. Jean Clark, remembered by fellow committee members for her wisdom, later spoke of parents' feelings:

> Horror and anger and – it was just a rebellious feeling that we had been let down so badly. We couldn't believe it. We expected a liberal report ... [recommending] community services and small homes, government support, but they didn't go that way at all ... the anger and hurt was intense. I think that must have been a tremendous blow to the Anyons because they had put

so much into the submissions and then to get this harsh report ... 'just put
them away'... we heard a rumour that they were saying, 'Oh, a colony over in
Norfolk Island would be a quite reasonable thing, and have an establishment
over there.' Based very much of course on the overseas big hospitals for handicapped people, which were then already being discounted by WHO [World
Health Organisation] reports, condemned by them.

The Consultative Committee acknowledged that conditions at Levin and
Templeton were not all they should be, but saw nothing inherently wrong with
the concept of mental deficiency colonies. In fact the government should build
more of the colonies: the 'mentally deficient' should not be left in mental
hospitals or kept at home.

Within weeks of the release of the Aitken Report the IHCPA held its fourth
annual conference. The association now had over 1000 members; representatives of 14 of the 16 branches attended this conference. Both the Minister of
Education (Algie) and the Minister of Health (Marshall) gave speeches, reflecting
the notably different attitudes of the respective departments. It became increasingly clear that the IHCPA would have more productive dealings with the
Department of Education than with the Department of Health. Whereas
Education had a long tradition of co-operating with parents over such matters
as schooling and was used to listening to parents' views, the Mental Hygiene
Division of the Department of Health had no such attitude or tradition.

The Minister of Education invited the IHCPA to comment on the Aitken
Report and a further submission was accordingly presented on 16 June 1953. Of
the Aitken Report's 10 recommendations, the IHCPA was particularly opposed
to numbers 2, 5 and 7. The second recommendation specified that institutions
cater for 400–500 people, and members urged that this be reduced to 200–250,
with greater decentralisation 'so that each district is adequately covered'. Delegates
also wanted greater subsidies to voluntary bodies that provided occupational
groups, cottage homes and senior occupational centres.

The IHCPA backed up its views with citations from a working paper from the
WHO's Joint Expert Committee on the Mentally Defective Child, plus letters
from other overseas experts opposed to large institutions. One of these experts
contacted by the association was a New Zealander, Dr J. Tizard, then living in
London. He was associated with the Medical Research Council Unit for
Research in Occupation Adaptation and also a consultant to the Joint Expert
Committee. The New Zealand IHCPA sent him a copy of the Aitken Report and
asked for his comments, which he sent in April 1953.

Keith Anyon, son of the founders of IHC, working for local bootmaker, Mr A. Ross, Khandallah, Wellington, early 1950s.

TO PARENTS AND GUARDIANS OF BACK-
WARD CHILDREN
IN WELLINGTON DISTRICT.

A MEETING will be held at the B.M.A
Rooms, 26 The Terrace, on Tuesday,
October 25, at 8pm.

Objects: To consider the formation of a
Parents' Association, which will link with
Associations in other Centres; to discuss the
Occupational Centre to be opened shortly at
Oriental Bay by the Education Board.

This meeting is convened by a group of
parents, and parents and guardians only are
invited.

Advertisement for the inaugural meeting, Evening Post, 22 October 1949.   IHC LIBRARY COLLECTION

First occupational centre in the cricket pavilion at the Basin Reserve, Wellington, 1950.   JOHN ASHTON

Parents Meeting - B.M.A Rooms, 26 The Terrace
Oct 26th   8. P.m.

1. Mrs. Morris   91 Freyberg St. Lyall Bay
2. Mr   ..   do.
3. Mrs. O.M Grenfell   28 Espin Cres. Karori
4. Mrs. E.M. Alcock   23 Plunket St. Kelburn
5. Mr. L.A. Brydone   18 Witako St. Lower H.
6. Mrs. M Brydone   do.
7. Mr. A.B Pownall   43 Matai Rd Hataitai
8. Mr. R Graves   88 Onslow Rd Khandal.
9. Mrs. B Graves   do
10. Mrs. P Osborne   9 Kim St. Khandallah
11. Mr. Outhwaite   22 Normanby St. Sth Well'
12. Mrs. E Englert.   31 Rose St. Wadestown
13. Mrs. E Harris   15 Hutt Rd Petone
14. Mrs. C. Browne   171 Main Rd Upper Hutt
15. Mr. Moss   41 Lincoln Av. Lower Hutt
16. Mrs Moss
17. Mrs. N.R Bisdee   14 Copeland St Lower Hutt
18. Mrs. McInnes   10 Hugh St. Newtown
19. Mrs. A.W Scoble   2 Highbury Cres. Kelburn
20. Mr. H.S Anyon   16 Everest St Khandallah
21. Mrs. H.S Anyon   do .   do.
22. Mrs. Gladys Howell - 158 Russell Tce Newtown
23. (Mr Outhwaite phone 24-069) (8 till 5). Newtown

List of attendees at the inaugural meeting, 25 October 1949, BMA Rooms, 26 The Terrace, Wellington. IHC LIBRARY COLLECTION

44 Jellicoe Street, Wanganui East, 1950: thought to be the first home for children with an intellectual disability in New Zealand.   IHC LIBRARY COLLECTION

Opening of Kristina Home, Silverstream, Upper Hutt: H.S. Anyon (right) with J.R. Marshall, Minister of Health, 1954. H.S. Anyon was founding president, Intellectually Handicapped Children's Parents' Association, 1949.   EASTBOURNE STUDIOS

Sleeping porch, Kristina Home, Silverstream, Upper Hutt.   IHC LIBRARY COLLECTION

Christopher House, hostel, Hamilton, opened 1954.   IHC LIBRARY COLLECTION

Father Christmas visits Keith and Margaret Anyon at their home in Khandallah, Wellington. Margaret Anyon was founding secretary, Intellectually Handicapped Children's Parents' Association, 1949.   C.P.S. BOYER

Fundraising in the early days: Margaret Anyon (right).   DOMINION

Margaret Anyon (centre), Mrs G. Rowe (left) and Mrs Gerard at the third annual conference, 1952.

> The report is, I think, in some ways a disappointing document and I wonder if some of the recommendations express the most enlightened views on the subject. In particular I felt serious misgivings about the recommendations ... that all imbecile and idiot children whose parents can be persuaded to part with them should be persuaded to part with them 'at about the age of 5'. This seems to me to be crude and ill considered and indeed a somewhat dangerous recommendation. Diagnosis at the age of five is by no means accurate and the prognosis is often extremely uncertain at that age. I think too that in the report far too little attention has been paid to the possibility of providing in the community adequate assistance, both material and financial, to parents of imbecile children who live at home.

Dr Tizard believed that children should not be placed in institutions if it could be avoided but should be kept at home, where they received the affection and attention necessary for emotional and intellectual growth. In any case New Zealand would probably never have enough institutions to house all cases from the age of five even if it wanted to. No other country had ever managed to do so.

Before the release of the Aitken Report the New Zealand Committee of the IHCPA in Wellington had met with the Minister of Education and asked if the government would subsidise money raised by the association's branches to buy properties. The Minister advised that nothing could be done in the meantime. The New Zealand Committee sent out a circular to branches on 'Property Purchases' instructing that they defer any purchases until 'after the Consultative Committee has issued its findings'. Branches should confine themselves to using rented premises in the meantime.

Members debated hotly the relative merits of hostels and occupational centres. On the second day of the 1953 conference the New Zealand Committee presented the delegates with a 'Future Policy' proposal. Branch delegates agreed that rather than rushing in to provide costly services, the 16 branches would concentrate on building up membership and setting up services that the Government financed in total (occupational centres) or in part (occupational groups), or which didn't require property purchase (senior occupational centres, home aids).

It was resolved that occupational schools in the four main cities would cater for between 13 and 40 children. Occupational centres in larger provincial towns would cater for between eight and 13 children; occupational groups in rural areas would cater for between two and seven children.

Government subsidies were sufficient to provide only half a day per week of operation, but by a variety of means (stalls, street collections, raffles, working parties) members raised money to extend the periods of operation. By July 1953 the branches had set up 13 occupational groups catering for a total of 119 children, with numbers growing all the time.

Another paper for delegates at the 1953 conference contained proposals as to minimum requirements for various services: cottage homes, setting up a trust company, occupational groups, senior occupational centres and short-stay homes.

Mental Health Amendment Act 1954

The Mental Health Amendment Act 1954 brought little change. In line with the Consultative Committee's view it endorsed mental defective colonies as the best place for such children. The government planned to add more villas to Templeton and Levin. It allowed short-stay homes but not hostels. Education facilities would continue to be available in the community. The Health Minister took credit for the establishment of occupational centres and groups, neglecting to mention the IHCPA's part. The main change in the act was to introduce the term 'intellectually handicapped', and to rename mental defective colonies mental health colonies.

On 20 November 1954 the IHCPA convened a special meeting of the New Zealand Council in Hamilton to discuss the Mental Health Amendment Act. The council unanimously passed a resolution expressing 'grave concern and disapproval at the shortcomings and omissions' of the act.

Meanwhile the New Zealand Committee in Wellington was still negotiating with the Minister of Education to increase government subsidies. A deputation sought assistance for groups, refresher courses for instructors, travelling teachers to visit groups in small towns and specialised instruction for teachers in training. The Minister sent a paper on the subject to the 1955 conference, outlining seven proposals that can be summarised thus:

1. Reducing the minimum roll for an occupational centre from 16 to 12.
2. Reducing the minimum roll for an occupational group from six to five, and increasing the subsidy and opening hours to five half-days per week for groups.
3. Staffing of occupational centres should be:

12–20 pupils: 1 certificated teacher, 1 helper;

21–30 pupils: 1 certificated teacher, 2 helpers;

31–40 pupils: 1 certificated teacher, 3 helpers.

4. A teacher appointed to an occupational centre should be given a period of training under an experienced teacher.

5. The Correspondence School should continue with its work for handicapped children.

6. More accurate diagnosis and assessment of mental deficiency should be attempted by means of specialist clinics in the main centres.

7. Experimental research into the causes of mental defect could not be undertaken in New Zealand as the country was too small and any research should be directed to the study of 'carefully prepared case records with a view to continuing improvements in the handling of intellectually handicapped children'.

The first four proposals, while not as much as the IHCPA had hoped for, were an improvement on existing conditions. The last three were in effect a restatement of the existing position.

The conference agreed to accept the Minister's proposals and lobby for more subsidies for senior occupational centres operating in Auckland, Christchurch, Hawke's Bay, Wanganui, Petone and Dunedin. These subsidies were not forthcoming until 1956, when up to 50 per cent was given on the capital cost of approved buildings and furniture.

Despite being advised by the New Zealand Committee to stick to using rented accommodation, Wanganui, Hawke's Bay and South Auckland branches all went ahead and bought properties with money from donations.

Formation of the Branches

Wanganui

Established on 28 October 1950 using YMCA premises, the Wanganui branch was the first to purchase a property for use as an emergency home and occupational centre. In 1967 the branch opened Alma Gardens, a new workshop and day-care centre, and acquired a site for a hostel. By the late 1960s the branch had commissioned a new 46-bed hostel at Castlecliff – at the time the biggest of its kind in New Zealand. It was completed by the end of 1970 and ready for occupancy in early 1971.

A Rangitikei sub-branch was formed at a meeting in Marton in 1960. In 1990 this sub-branch joined together with the Feilding sub-branch of the Manawatu branch to form the Rangitikei branch.

Hawke's Bay

One of the first branches formed, Hastings opened a centre in May 1951. Hawke's Bay was represented at all the early New Zealand committee meetings. In May 1952 the branch paid a deposit on a property (Fairhaven) in Hastings and launched a fundraising campaign to raise the money to buy it for use as an occupational centre. In January 1956 a separate Napier branch came into being. At that stage Napier children were transported twice a week to attend the occupation centre in Hastings. In June 1965 after discussion with the Crippled Children's Society the Napier branch undertook to run a workshop planned and started by CCS. An agreement was signed between the branch and the Disabled Servicemen's Re-establishment League to use their building. Fairhaven School in Hastings was officially opened by the Education Department in September 1958.

For a year or two the Hastings branch lapsed into non-activity, to be revitalised in 1963 when 50 parents met to create a new Hastings branch. The following year came the first East Coast regional meeting of delegates from Hastings, Napier, Wairoa and Gisborne branches. In 1965 Hastings branch hosted the annual conference, which was attended by 94 delegates and observers.

A Central Hawke's Bay sub-group was established in 1966 with Pat Kilkolly as its first chairman and its occupation group initiated in part by Charles Waigth. He and his family had moved to Takapau in 1965 and first joined the Hastings branch, where they were made welcome by branch stalwarts the Hutchinsons. Concerned that the Hastings facility was too far away for their daughter Catherine to travel to, the Waigths worked with others to provide a facility in Waipawa. They obtained the free use of the county council buildings in Ruataniwha Street, Waipawa. Four women took the group: G. Davey, D. Pethwick, D. Bell and J. Logan.

Pahiatua–Woodville sub-branch set up their occupational group in Woodville in 1968 in the old Woodlands Road School. It was supported by the Lions Club. The Arahura Group was its first facility, with Lois Bradley as supervisor.

Auckland

The Auckland branch officially came into being on 24 July 1950 at a meeting attended by 180 parents. Officers elected were: E.S. Woolley (president), C. Luker (vice-president), Mrs B. Gordon (hon. secretary) and Mrs G.C. Park (hon. treasurer). Committee members were Mrs Benseman, Mrs Avery, Mr Bell and Mr Smith. The committee met two weeks later to discuss plans for a residential school in Auckland for the intellectually handicapped. The committee inspected a property in Drury but the scheme was later dropped.

The following year, on 10 September 1951, members met to discuss plans for an occupational group in Otahuhu, which had its first session on 13 November. Four children attended at first, transported in a small bus by Mrs Doyle from Mondays to Thursdays from 9.30am to 2.30pm. It was only the beginning. The Otahuhu Centre committee under Mr Purdie made an application to the government to form an occupational school under the control of the Auckland Education Board.

In June 1952 a senior occupational group for ten 13-year-olds was established and met in the Pitt Street Methodist Church Hall. Four months later, by which time there were 14 trainees, alternative accommodation was found at St Stephen's Presbyterian church. In November the same year an occupational group was established in Pukekohe with nine pupils under the supervision of Mrs Jowsey. On 16 May 1953 the Auckland branch, with the help of Rotary, purchased a property (Edithville) at 17 Symonds Street, which was opened by the mayor of Auckland on 30 July 1955.

In December 1953 the Auckland branch recorded:

> We have three minor groups established and an 18 plus centre which is the topic of discussion at this time ... we see boys and girls who never had the opportunity before of becoming self-reliant, learning to read, write and take their place in the community and we as parents marvel at the possibilities ... Only a short time ago all the pupils were gathered together by taxis, now some of them travel all the way alone while others travel by the public transport system under little supervision. The school is open from 9.00am to 1.00pm four days weekly and 20 girls and boys sparkle with delight in an environment that prevents them from being looked upon as social outcasts with no potentialities of ever being useful citizens. The supervisor, Mr Clayton, is the man behind the development and his patience and understanding is responsible for the accomplishments ... A sub-committee comprising parents now controls the centre on behalf of the branch.

In June 1980 the Auckland branch opened the Otahuhu Hostels in Avenue Road: the first residential units to be established in the Auckland branch area. The homes were specially designed to provide a homely environment with attached accommodation for staff. They came about largely through the efforts of Cliff Benson of Mangere, George Hardy of Otahuhu and Mrs I. Lehmann of Papatoetoe.

A separate North Shore branch was formed in 1953 and a North Shore occupational group was formed at a meeting in May 1953, opening in September that year with five children. Mrs Kearney was the supervisor.

1957: Western suburbs group formed.

1958: Southern suburbs group formed and purchased a property at 28 Albion Road, Otahuhu, which was sold in 1964.

1961: Edithville sold and a property at 56 Ranfurly Road purchased. One-time branch president Don Wills later wrote: 'I feel that the Branch came of age when the decision was made to proceed with the Ranfurly road complex. When it was commissioned, planning was already in hand for the extensions – finally the Hostel of which we were all so proud.' Ranfurly House Hostel opened in 1973.

1974: Pre-school centre (Fitzgerald) for the eastern suburbs opened. Manukau sub-branch was set up in 1974 and opened a centre in a church hall in Papatoetoe the following year. At the time it was the only facility in the Otara–Papatoetoe–Mangere area. Otara special-care centre opened in June 1977 and five years later in 1982 a pre-school junior centre was opened in Dawson Road, Otara. It was named the Waigth Centre in recognition of the work of Charlie Waigth, formerly of Hawke's Bay and for many years a driving force in the Manukau sub-branch. The centre was built to accommodate 40 intellectually handicapped children with an average teacher-child ratio of one to four.

Thames/Hauraki became a sub-branch of Auckland in the 1960s.

South Auckland/Waikato

Lorna Ranby was first president of the South Auckland branch, which was formed in August 1950. She was a dedicated worker for IHC, visiting families in any spare time she had. Her daughter remembers: 'Every night after tea our Mother would disappear and we never knew if she would come home.'

A Waikato member recalled that in 1949 she and her husband had responded to the advertisement asking for parents to make contact. She said it took some time for members of the new branch to feel the benefits of belonging to the association, but the IHCPA raised feelings of hope and security for the future. 'Raising funds for all these homes [to provide for children] in old age, this was their dream – I mean, all the parents dreamt that the IHC would "look after my boy when I die."'

Christopher House was named after the son of the Ranbys in recognition of their work. This first IHC hostel, providing short-stay accommodation, was opened in Hamilton East by Dame Hilda Ross on 24 April 1954.

Iris Skelton, who had a daughter with Down's Syndrome, remembered the early years at Christopher House. After an interview with Lorna Ranby she was invited to take the position as matron. Admissions soon reached the maximum of 12 residents aged from four years upwards. Their handicaps included Down's Syndrome, autism and hearing disabilities, and others were awaiting psychological assessment. Every weekday the residents walked to a church hall in Grey Street a few blocks away for playgroup activities: singing, games, socialising.

Later that year the South Auckland group opened a full occupational centre at 128 Clarence Street, with the necessary minimum of 16 children. Several women offered to become a 'mother help' in the new occupational centre or sat on knitting and chatting to other mothers while their children joined in the programmes. The few hours a week of respite care provided by the occupational centre was therapeutic for everyone: enjoyable, constructive and confidence building.

Eventually the Clarence Street Occupational Centre, funded and staffed by the South Auckland Education Board, was made available to children from Christopher House and others from the Hamilton area. Meanwhile the branch had also bought land in Morrinsville Road, Hillcrest, and went ahead with another major project: a hostel and other facilities in a complex known as Christopher Park. Iris Skelton's daughter Jenny, then aged 18, was one of the first to enjoy the privilege of attending an IHC workshop. Iris was matron at Christopher House until 1960, and served on the executive committee from 1963 to 1969 and from 1978 to 1981.

Sub-branches were formed throughout the area in the 1950s at Huntly, Ngaruawahia, Taumarunui, Otorohanga, Te Kuiti, Te Awamutu, Tokoroa, Putaruru, Te Aroha and Waihi. King Country became a full branch in 1976. Bruce and Pat Howell were among those responsible for setting it up.

Franklin

In October 1952 Franklin broke away from the Auckland branch and became a separate entity.

Waikato South/Matamata

In July 1954 the mayor of Matamata presided over a special meeting to raise funds for the Matamata Intellectually Handicapped Children's Parents' Association. Guest speaker Lorna Ranby outlined plans for a suitable home for training people with intellectual handicaps. This meeting set up a small committee to organise a house-to-house collection while the Country Women's Institute and Women's Division of Federated Farmers helped collect donations from Walton to Tirau. Within a month a cheque for £300 was forwarded to Lorna and the committee continued to raise funds for the IHCPA.

It was not until September 1962 that the Matamata sub-branch held its first AGM, presided over by Dr Stone. Norman Cashmore, the first president, and his committee successfully sought support from the Lions Club to organise and build a day-care centre, which was officially opened on 8 February 1971. By 1989 Matamata had a vocational centre and residential home and the Education Board had built a special school adjacent to the day-care centre.

Iris Skelton moved from Hamilton to Morrinsville and became a very active member of the Waikato South branch. She became a life member in 1982 and died in 1989.

Northland

Meynell Strathmore Blomfield was one of those responsible for setting up the Whangarei branch in 1952. Known as Lofty, Blomfield, born in 1908, had played representative rugby before making a career for himself as a wrestler with an international reputation. When war broke out in 1939 he served overseas with the New Zealand 21st Battalion. Back in New Zealand he married and moved to Northland to manage the Whangarei Hotel. In 1948 his first child, a girl, was born with an intellectual disability and this had a profound effect on his thinking. His energy and commitment to the cause, and that of Dr Donald Beasley, meant that from its inception this branch was extremely active. Lofty was also a huge drawcard for any publicity and fundraising efforts.

Some of these endeavours were a little unorthodox and for a few years caused a rift between Blomfield and the Anyons, but it was later smoothed over. Notable was his 'penny pile' on the bar of his hotel, which grew to mammoth proportions.

In 1955 the branch purchased a spacious old house in Maunu Road with four acres of land, within half a mile of the Whangarei shopping area. It was opened as St Nicholas Hostel that year.

Northland hosted the annual conference in 1961 in the premises of the intermediate school, with three local hotels providing free accommodation for delegates. During the conference a new hostel and occupation centre were opened. From that time one of the chief activities of the branch was the sheltered workshop.

Sub-branches were set up in Dargaville and Kaikohe.

An exciting development for IHC in Northland came with the bequest by Alice McCardle to the branch of a beach property at McKenzie's Bay near the Whangarei Heads. The branch developed the house into a holiday home, opened in 1967.

Tauranga

Originally an Auckland sub-branch, the Tauranga branch was constituted in 1961 and within a few years opened a 20-bed hostel. Tauranga hosted the 1973 annual conference.

Te Puke

Te Puke started a branch at a meeting in 1955 of what the journal described as a 'small, sad group' of people. 'At that time the loneliness and dismay of the unexpected was an intolerable burden to them. Few people knew their children with an intellectual disability, spoke to them or of them, except in the high-pitched voice of the self-conscious righteous.'

At the outset the branch provided a school for 23 children in the local basketball pavilion. Within five months, with the significant aid and unflagging support of Rotary and Jaycees, the branch had built the 900 square foot school. By 1989 it had also established two beautiful residential homes.

Rotorua

Rotorua group was set up in 1950 as part of the South Auckland branch and had a separate committee from 1955. The branch came into being in 1961 and in due course sub-branches were established in Taupo and Turangi. In 1963 Rotorua opened Awhina, which was later sold and three new villas built.

Gisborne/East Coast/Eastern Bay of Plenty

The Gisborne branch was formed in 1951, with Wairoa as a sub-branch. Wairoa became a full branch in 1964. Gisborne opened a hostel in 1969.

Whakatane, formed as a sub-branch in July 1961, was elevated to branch status in 1964 through the efforts of members of the Women's Division of Federated Farmers. The same year the branch set up an occupational centre for 12 children between the ages of five and 18 years, in the Citizens' Band Hall in Francis Street, Whakatane. Daphne Regan, the teacher employed by the Education Department, remembers the change in outlook that occurred in the mid-sixties regarding education for children with intellectual handicaps. Special schools built by the government brought the responsibility for education for all children under one umbrella. In February that year Daphne Regan opened an opportunity workshop, starting with three workers and a small group of dedicated voluntary helpers but with plans to accommodate 20 people. In 1976, after an interim move, the centre and workshop, known as the Adult Training Centre, moved into its own building in Alexander Avenue.

Opotiki, a sub-branch of Whakatane, was formed in 1967. Trainees from there and Kawerau were sent on a daily basis to the centre in Whakatane.

Taranaki

The North Taranaki branch at New Plymouth had an initial meeting in December 1950 and officially came into being in February 1951. The branch opened a new opportunity workshop in 1967 and hosted the 1979 annual conference.

South Taranaki

This branch was formed from an initial meeting held in the Hawera Borough

Chambers in August 1959. Hawera Occupational Centre, later to be named Awhine, opened on 29 May 1961 with two teachers. The modern spacious building was erected by the Taranaki Education Board and comprised two large classrooms, toilets, a modern kitchen, staffroom and a toolshed.

Wellington

The Wellington branch opened a senior centre in the RSA Hall at Petone on 30 May 1953. In March that year the committee was given first option on the T.A. Duncan Polio Hospital at Silverstream: a building with 20 rooms and large grounds. As the price was well beyond its means the branch asked the government for help, but by the time the Health Department was prepared to make a decision the property was on the general market and it appeared that all hope was gone. Then came wonderful news. A benefactor had bought the hospital and would let the Wellington branch have the use of it for a nominal rent. It was later revealed that the donor was C.H.R. (Dick) Jepsen, from whom the government had bought the site for the Coromandel Street occupational centre. He was the business partner of Jean Clark's husband Gilbert Clark, and was interested in the work of the IHCPA. The Wellington branch agreed to administer the property under the terms of a trust set up by Dick Jepsen. The hospital was renamed the Kristina Home for IHC (after Jepsen's late wife) and was to provide short-stay accommodation only.

The Wellington branch now had a property, but had to find money to run it. Hal Anyon wrote to the Minister of Health:

> We should be glad to know what help we may expect departmentally to meet our running costs. Each child who remains outside a State Institution reduces the cost of maintenance accepted by the State when parents must send the child permanently away from home ...'

After much discussion, in March 1954 came a major breakthrough. Jack Marshall as Minister had always claimed to have sympathy with the association, especially for mothers 'burdened by the constant care and attention which most intellectually handicapped children require'. He announced that the government had decided it would assist the IHCPA:

> Cabinet has approved in principle the granting to the IHCPA of a subsidy of up to 50% on the capital cost of approved buildings and hard furniture acquired for the purpose of providing short stay homes for I.H. children ...

Cabinet has also decided that a subsidy of 6/- per day per bed occupied by children under 16 years of age in these homes should be paid to the Association.

Kristina Home was opened by the Minister on 24 April 1954. In 1962 the Wellington branch purchased property at Keepa Street, Levin, for the use of parents visiting their children at Levin Hospital and Training School. Named Kimberley House, it opened in April that year.

Otago

One of the earliest to be established, the Dunedin-based Otago branch elected R.W.S. (Stan) Botting as president when it first met in December 1949. A second public meeting was held in the Dunedin YWCA buildings on 5 February 1950.

The Hunterville Hostel in Dunedin was destroyed by fire in the late 1950s and the Education Department, reluctant to rebuild, negotiated with the Otago branch to take over responsibility for Hunterville and meanwhile use Kew Home, opened in 1958, not only for short-stay purposes but also for the hostel accommodation of the country children who had been attending Hunterville and the centre at Sara Cohen School.

Southland

Based in Invercargill, Southland was also one of the first branches formed. It later had sub-branches at Gore, Tuatapere, Riverton, Otautau, Mataura and Bluff. Tom Brydone and his family moved to Gore in the early 1950s and enrolled daughter Maryann with the IHC in Invercargill, where she joined an occupational centre.

Soon after its inception, Southland began planning a new centre and home for which considerable funding was required. The branch organised a massive fundraising campaign which included in April 1964 a very successful radio appeal. The amount raised, £32,500, was beyond any expectations. Kindhaven, the new 36-bed hostel, at a total cost of $200,000, was opened in Invercargill on 18 September 1967 by Lady Fergusson, wife of Governor General Sir Bernard Fergusson.

Canterbury

A motivating force behind the setting up of the Canterbury branch on 1 June 1950, was that the Education Department had advised that pupils over 18 years could no longer attend occupational centres. As there were several over this age attending the Christchurch occupational centre there was an urgent need to make alternative provision for these people.

The first recorded meeting of parents, guardians and others interested in IHC was held in the ACC Rooms. Mr Fanning was elected president of the occupational centre committee and the meeting was attended by 160 people including doctors, psychologists, teachers and friends. Tom Brydone, treasurer of the Wellington committee of the IHCPA, was guest speaker. The second meeting held on 2 August 1950 and attended by 73 people, elected a committee: J. Keenan (president), M. Tucker (vice-president), N. Thomas (treasurer), F. Fanning (secretary) and a committee of six.

The first general meeting of the Canterbury IHCPA was held on 2 November 1950, attended by 26 people. A year later F.A. Hallam took over as president, concerned that the IHCPA had so far done nothing for the 18-plus age group, although this had been one of the main reasons for its formation. In Christchurch, most adults with a disability could not get into the sheltered workshop and there was nothing for them to do. Eventually a part-time group was started by Mrs Love in a room provided by the Durham Street Methodist church.

After an enthusiastic beginning, parents' interest fell away and had reached a very low level when S.A. Roberts was elected president in 1955. From then on steady progress was made both in membership and finance. Mrs McLachlan remembers that the highlight of the later 1950s was the purchase and development of a property in Worcester Street, which was opened by the Minister of Health.

South Canterbury

This branch was formed in 1951 with its headquarters in Timaru. Similar steps were taken in Ashburton which, initially a sub-branch of Christchurch, became a full branch in 1965. South Canterbury opened a 10-bed hostel in 1966.

North Canterbury

The hard work of Des Moore, Leith Sloss and others saw a North Canterbury branch established in 1987. Rita Moore was the first staff member of their residential facilities, which 10 years later numbered three homes, child and family support, a day service and an employment programme.

Nelson

On 28 September 1953, only four years after the association was formed, the Nelson group became a branch. A first priority was establishing an occupational centre. Parents and later the Nelson Jaycees worked to create a busy and active centre, and annual street-day appeals helped raise money for activities. The 16th branch, Nelson hosted the 1964 annual conference.

Buller/Westland

With headquarters at Westport, Buller was an early starter but in the mid-1950s went into recess. However, through the interest of Dr McDougall of the Department of Health a Westland branch was formed in a church hall in Greymouth in 1959, serving the vast area from Karamea in the north to the Haast in the south. Shortly after its formation the parents began occupational group activities and moved to larger premises. Donations from the Sutherland Self Help Trust Fund and service clubs enabled the branch to purchase new premises for a group centre, which was officially opened by local MP Paddy Blanchfield on 1 February 1964.

Marlborough

In Blenheim, Mrs Williamson, a speech therapist, noticed in the course of her work that there were several intellectually handicapped children in the Marlborough district and a visit by IHCPA president Stan Botting resulted in the formation of the Marlborough branch in 1961. As with most branches, fundraising was a high priority to help with finances and also raise the profile of the branch in the community.

North Otago

In 1962 the North Otago branch was formed with headquarters at Oamaru and according to Stan Botting was the only branch that initiated the three services within a short time of formation: pre-school, occupational centre and a senior workshop.

Growing Pains: The Anyons Depart

In June 1954 Hal Anyon announced that he thought the IHCPA should get up another petition and appeal to Parliament. He wanted more consideration of the question of 'cottage homes' and government subsidies. Others on the New Zealand Committee disagreed with the idea and a fiery meeting ensued. Voices were raised and tempers lost, with the upshot that the New Zealand Committee rejected the Anyons' idea in favour of continued discussions with the Minister of Health. It was becoming known that because of their rather notorious methods, some politicians were refusing to deal with the Anyons.

By then it was too late to affect the Mental Health Amendment Act, but on 21 September 1954 Hal Anyon (and nine others) went ahead and presented a private petition. This action, timed to coincide with the lead-up to the general election, widened the rift that had already appeared between the Anyons and the New Zealand Committee. The Anyons felt that the committee was being too conciliatory and complacent about the expansion of the mental institutions.

Another controversial issue at the time was a proposal to open up the membership of the association to non-parents. The Anyons vehemently opposed this proposal.

The following year the Anyons stormed out of the annual conference. It was later claimed that Hal Anyon had to be physically removed from the chair by Gus Nichol when Stan Botting was elected president. The Anyons formally resigned from their executive positions in the Wellington branch on 2 May 1955, writing:

> It is obvious to us that a new phase in the life of our association has been
> entered and for some time in the past influences that have been instrumental
> in introducing this new phase have also played a part in determining our
> decision to retire from the active work of the Association and particularly

from the Branch. The future of the Association will for some time be affected by this new phase of development.

Harold Anyon had already by this time resigned from the Kristina Home committee but he and Margaret, though no longer involved with the IHC executive, continued to be very active in the movement. They were called, along with the nine other petitioners, to state their case before the Public Health Committee on 7 September 1955. Their submission concentrated on the need for suitable homes, not institutions, for 'adult handicapped children'. They asked for the law to be amended to allow 'private approved organisations' to set up homes for such children. The Public Health Committee reported on the petition to the House on 22 September advising that in their opinion the petitioners' recommendations 'receive favourable consideration'.

It was probably inevitable that the Anyons would no longer feel happy with the IHCPA. It had been started as their baby, and a small and very successful militant protest group. Now, because of its success, the IHC was a larger, more formal and professional organisation. It is also likely that people in the more remote branches resented the Wellington domination of the organisation. Far from the capital, they had only the vaguest idea of what the Anyons had done, and did not or could not appreciate the extent of their achievement. But what they had achieved with their passionate commitment, energy, hard work and knowledge of how the system worked in those early years for people with an intellectual disability and their families was of inestimable value not just to the people involved but to New Zealand as a whole. As someone commented, 'I doubt that anyone else could have done quite what they did.'

Stan Botting later recorded that the IHC owed to the Anyons 'a debt that can never be repaid or even fully appreciated. The moral courage shown and their complete devotion to the cause of the intellectually handicapped must rank high in the annals of social service.'

3

Unremitting Endeavour

A New Approach

The newly elected president was Robert William Stanley (Stan) Botting, then aged 62, a master at Otago Boys' High School and World War I veteran. He and his wife Mary, married in 1920, had four children and David, the youngest, was born in 1931 with Down's Syndrome. Mary refused to accept advice to put her child into a home, and David was brought up with the family, attending a special class and later an occupational centre. When the Otago branch was formed, it was Mary Botting who pushed husband Stan into becoming branch chair and then national president. Throughout his years of involvement Stan always had the support of Mary, who accompanied him everywhere. It was a long and trying journey from Dunedin to Wellington in those days, involving a whole day in a train and a night on the ferry. The position of president was almost a full-time job, which was made easier for Stan once he had retired from teaching.

The new president was a very different character from Hal Anyon. Like his predecessor, Stan Botting was a highly respected man of authority, but he had a quieter manner, and a wide experience and high reputation through his work with the Rugby Football Union, the Dunedin City Council and later the New

Zealand Electrical Supply Authority. Under Botting, the IHCPA was charac-
terised by a more conciliatory approach. By the early 1960s conference remits
were less radical than formerly, having been well and truly thrashed out at branch
level. As Botting observed: 'Older members may look back nostalgically to the
fiery enthusiasm of the early years but the quieter tone of today suggests that
we know for the most part where we want to go. But still we must be persistent.'

By contrast with the Anyons, Stan Botting regarded the opening of the
association to non-parents as 'the best thing we ever did'. One of the first such
people was Dr D.M.G. (Donald) Beasley, a paediatrician based in Whangarei
who had just returned from postgraduate studies in Britain. Then aged 35, he
was married with children, but his interest in people with intellectual disability
came from his specialist work in paediatrics. He helped form the Northland
branch of the association.

A fortunate appointment in 1956 during the Botting term of office was that
of R.G. (Ray) Mathews as general secretary. A qualified accountant and senior
partner in a Wellington firm of chartered accountants, Mathews was also a
lecturer at Victoria University College. The days when the paperwork for the
society was done on the Anyon kitchen table were now ancient history. Mathews
brought a much-needed expertise and professionalism to a society with a rapidly
growing membership and increasingly complex finances. During his long involvement with the association he showed resourcefulness, commitment and business
acumen far beyond any material compensation the society could give. Ray
Mathews was awarded a Churchill Fellowship in 1972 and relinquished the
position of general secretary in 1977.

In July 1957 when the government was considering amendments to the Mental
Health Act it invited the IHCPA to make a submission. The amendment when
passed met most of their requests. Clause 11 extended the permissible length of
stay in a short-stay home to three months, though this did not apply to children
over 18 years.

Clause 12 allowed the association (and other incorporated societies) to set up
licensed permanent homes for the care and training of intellectually handicapped
children over the age of 15 years. Though it had acquiesced to some of the
IHCPA's demands, the official government view remained that institutions
provided the best kind of long-term care for most of the intellectually handicapped. Both Levin and Templeton farm colonies increased in size during the
latter 1950s and 1960s.

The IHCPA now ceased to push for the abolition of the large institutions, conceding that under existing conditions the state institutions were necessary for some people with severe disabilities. Rather, members wanted the government to build new institutions and keep the existing ones from getting any larger. Auckland parents in particular were concerned that New Zealand's largest city had no mental deficiency institution. Children from the northern districts had to be sent either hundreds of miles away to Levin or to the nearer but less suitable Avondale and Kingseat mental hospitals.

Conditions in the institutions were improving, partly as a result of pressure from and efforts made by the IHCPA. Parents worked to improve facilities by sending toys, pictures and books to the institutions. They continued to ask for more training programmes for the children, more speech and occupational therapists to be appointed. They also wanted short-stay facilities.

In 1959 official 'visiting committees' were formed to monitor conditions for the disabled in institutions. Appointed were: Jean Clark, A. Alcock, G. Whyte, W. Minston and Olive Grenfell. When the Auckland branch presented a petition asking for the Mental Hygiene Division to establish an institution or 'home' for Auckland similar to those at Levin and Templeton, the government agreed and land for the new institution was found at Mangere. Although this was a significant step and the petition appeared to have succeeded in its aims, nothing further happened until 1964. Even after building began, progress was frustratingly slow.

The Burns Report

Confidence in the approach and viewpoint of the IHCPA received a major boost in 1959. Sir Charles Burns, who had been supportive to the Anyons and was widely regarded as sympathetic towards the aims and objects of IHCPA, headed a sub-committee of the New Zealand branch of the British Medical Association. It issued a report that was in many respects critical of government policy and the Aitken Report. The foreword criticised the policies as 'based on outworn and outmoded ideas'. Burns wrote that the Consultative Committee had 'failed in its purpose which was surely to recommend ways and means of improving the lot of the mentally subnormal child and it failed seemingly because it took no cognisance of what was going on in the world elsewhere'. The report quoted overseas research and emphasised the 'great danger of using a low IQ as an excuse for inaction rather than as a starting point for planned training and treatment'.

The sub-committee criticised the mental deficiency institutions as too custodial, too isolated and too large, and for placing insufficient emphasis on education, training and rehabilitation. It was particularly critical of the fact that 17 per cent of the first admissions between 1953 and 1956 were children under five years of age, and of these only 10 per cent were in the severest category of deficiency. 'High-grade' patients were being admitted too frequently and too young, when at an early age prognosis was uncertain. Some children diagnosed as mentally defective later improved and became self-supporting. Separation from the family at an early age often retarded intellectual development because the child missed the stimulation of a family environment, the sub-committee stated. Residential institutions where necessary should be small and made up of family-type units.

The report received considerable publicity. Stan Botting on behalf of the IHCPA told the press that the organisation was completely in accord with the Burns Report's recommendations. The government was less enthusiastic. H.G.R. Mason, Minister of Health, said: 'There is some truth in the ideas that have prompted the report, but there is extravagance in the over-optimistic picture presented in what may be achieved.' (*Evening Post*, 3 March 1959)

Dr Lewis, director of the Mental Hygiene Division, later was reported as saying that the government was 'not irrevocably committed to a policy of placing all mentally subnormal children in large institutions remote from the centres of population ... the policy of the Department for children with mild mental subnormality was to encourage voluntary bodies to make better provision for them.' (*Dominion*, 26 June 1959)

Following this report the government granted subsidies to IHCPA to establish and run certain services: occupational centres and short-stay homes. However the government also continued to concentrate on establishing large institutions for the severely disabled. Although the IHCPA agreed at the time that these institutions were necessary they believed that those planned by the government were too big.

It was clear, however, that the relationship between the IHCPA and the government had come a long way in a decade.

1955–1965: Decade of Steady Progress

Under Stan Botting's presidency the association progressed from being a pioneering protest group towards gaining establishment status – even respectability. The IHCPA saw itself as providing a voice for people with an intellectual disability and their parents, as well as being a welfare organisation concerned with providing services. New branches sprang up, membership increased to more than 1000. Venues for annual conferences rotated among the regions, with branches taking it in turn to act as host for them. Much hard work by members resulted in branches providing new day-care, occupational and short-stay facilities.

For a number of years the association had been fighting for the legal right to establish full residential facilities. Under the terms of the 1956 Amendment to the Mental Health Act an intellectually handicapped child could with departmental approval be admitted to a short-stay home for up to two months. An interval of six months must then intervene before a second application could be considered except in exceptional circumstances, and on this matter the department was apparently co-operative. A subsidy of six shillings a day was paid by the Health Department for those under 16 years when occupying beds in short-stay homes. An Invalid Benefit was available for those over 16 years and from this it was considered board could be paid. At the time this was a tremendous breakthrough for the association. Throughout the next few years a major thrust of the New Zealand Committee on behalf of its membership was to have government subsidies increased. Gains were slowly achieved. In 1963 history was made when concerns affecting the intellectually handicapped were mentioned in the Budget with the welcome news that the government subsidy had increased to 10 shillings per occupied bed per day.

Despite the work and significant progress made by the IHCPA, life for parents of handicapped children was not easy. Peter and Peg Hanan recall: 'Elaine was born in 1956. There was no "early intervention", no "parent to parent", no social workers and very little information.' The doctor at first kept the news from Elaine's parents and later instead of help there was 'a lot of ill-informed advice ... more fearful than encouraging'. In their rural district there was no schooling for Elaine and the IHC was in its infancy. Like so many parents with a disabled child the Hanans had only two choices: to move to an area where the services were more appropriate or to set to work and develop services. And like so many others the Hanans went ahead and 'did it themselves'. As time went on the IHC gave more support to parents when they started a school group in the local town. 'We supposed that this was an achievement but it was only one hurdle. Perhaps we were fortunate that we could not see the future problems ahead,' recalls Peg.

1960 was proclaimed World Mental Health Year and it was heartening for New Zealand members to discover what progress was being made, if any, in other countries. To realise that their problems were shared by parents in all parts of the world, in all walks of life. They learnt, for example, that President and Mme de Gaulle of France and President Kennedy of the United States had family members with an intellectual handicap.

The 1960 annual conference endorsed a proposal to provide funding to enable Dr Donald Beasley (then with the Mental Hygiene Division) to attend the International Conference on Mental Deficiency in London. While overseas he travelled widely in England, Europe and North America studying programmes for adults with an intellectual disability and visiting a variety of facilities for the intellectually disabled. On his return Dr Beasley toured New Zealand giving talks to IHC branches. He also wrote a number of articles that parents found inspirational, focussing on in particular the concept of sheltered workshops.

The 1962 conference endorsed a move to turn the 'senior centres' into workshops to train some older children to go into the workforce and to provide continuing employment for others. The trainees/employees would earn a small amount of money and gain self-esteem and independence.

The same period had seen the passing of the Disabled Persons Employment Promotion Act (1960). The association informed members that 'under this Act any organisation such as ours may be granted exemption from the Acts mentioned [including the Factories Act] so that they may legally run sheltered workshops'. By 1969, as well as day-care centres and hostels, IHCPA branches ran 20 workshops catering for 480 adults.

That year the government agreed to provide 50 per cent salary subsidies for approved staff in opportunity workshops. One of those employed was Trish Coulthard. From her home in Lower Hutt she was taken every weekday by bus to the sheltered workshop in Naenae. The work was full time and involved packing such things as supply packs for the New Zealand Army, for which she was paid the equivalent of 5 shillings per week on top of her invalid benefit.

A New Journal

It was in 1960 also that the association established its journal: replacing news-letters, which had tended to look amateurish, appeared spasmodically and always lapsed. While many of the branches published their own newsletters, conference had requested that the association appoint an editor and produce a professional publication. The result was the attractively presented *The Intellectually Handi-capped Child: official journal of the New Zealand Intellectually Handicapped Children's Parents' Association Inc.* The inaugural issue, dated spring 1960, was edited by F.W. Ashton, who was succeeded by C.R. Monigatti. From that time onwards the association had a major outlet for news about branch and membership activities, and issues of national importance, research and treatment of disabling conditions and aspects of relevant new legislation.

The Mental Health Amendment Act (1961) was a case in point. The journal informed members:

> Since January 1, 1962, parents wishing to have their children admitted to any of the Division of Mental Health hospitals are no longer required to do this by way of certification. Clause 6 of the Mental Health Amendment Act provides for the informal admission of mentally subnormal persons (a term which includes not only the intellectually handicapped but also the somewhat higher groups commonly known hitherto as feeble-minded).

The association was jubilant about the passing of the Education Act (1964) and the Department of Education's decision to assume responsibility for the education of children with an intellectual disability. Staffing and the full opera-tional costs would be met of occupational groups with a minimum roll of five children. This freed parents to direct some of their efforts to senior occupational centres for those over 18 years of age, hostels (including short-stay facilities) day-care and special care centres.

President Botting wrote that it had taken the New Zealand Committee more than 10 years of unremitting endeavour to convince the education authorities 'that our children were entitled under a free and compulsory system of education to have equality of treatment with their more fortunate brethren'. At the time the Education Act (1964) appeared as a significant breakthrough; it was only later that members became fully aware of the act's shortcomings and limitations.

A New Name

In 1962 at the annual conference in Timaru the association adopted a new name, the Intellectually Handicapped Children's Society. The change reflected the new direction its philosophy had taken. That year important administrative changes also came about when co-opted non-parent member Dr Donald Beasley became vice-president and at his suggestion the society was restructured into a regional scheme. While the branches were retained, New Zealand was divided into regions or zones, each of which could nominate a member (or two members) to sit on the New Zealand Committee. Until then the New Zealand Committee had consisted of six committee members as well as the president and vice-president and with the growth in numbers of branches, this meant that many branches were not represented, including some of the largest. The conference adopted a proposal providing for 10 regions:

> Northern: including all of Northland
> Auckland: Auckland, North Shore and Franklin
> South Auckland: South Auckland branch
> Bay of Plenty: Tauranga, Rotorua and Eastern Bay of Plenty (Whakatane and Opotiki)
> East Coast: Gisborne, Wairoa, Napier and Hastings
> Midland: Taranaki, South Taranaki, Taihape, Wanganui, Manawatu and Rangitikei
> Central: Wairarapa, Wellington, Nelson and Marlborough
> Canterbury: West Coast and Canterbury, South Canterbury, Ashburton
> Otago: Otago province
> Southland: Southland branch, Invercargill

At the 1964 conference, hosted by the Nelson branch, Stan Botting stepped down from the presidency. Members presented the Bottings with a coffee service in gratitude for their many years of work for the society, and Dr Beasley read a tribute to the retiring president.

> We remember him for his infinite patience in those frustrating early days when his kindly restraining hand was vitally necessary in preserving harmony. At all times he was cheerful and optimistic; some little gain was the cause for rejoicing, but not an excuse for relaxing. He pursued those points which he considered vital to the progress of our movement with persistence yet with an honesty of purpose which gained for him the full confidence of those with

IHC pre-school, Kawerau.   RUTH GERZON

SPRING, 1960.

the **I**ntellectually **H**andicapped **IH CHILD**

Registered at the G.P.O. Wellington as a Magazine.

Official Journal of the
New Zealand
Intellectually Handicapped Children's Parents
Association Incorporated

The first issue of the official journal of the New Zealand Intellectually Handicapped Children's Parents'
Association Inc.

JB Munro, Southland branch administrator, accepts a cot from St John's Ambulance cadets, Invercargill, 1968.

Lorna Ranby, the pioneer whose drive and passion laid the foundations of South Auckland branch.   IHC LIBRARY COLLECTION

Jack Tizard, Professor of Child Development, University of London, who, with the IHCPA, condemned the inadequacies and shortcomings of the Aitken Report, 1953.
IHC LIBRARY COLLECTION

R.W.S. Botting, national president IHC 1954–64, at the annual conference 1978, Nelson.
IHC LIBRARY COLLECTION

M.S. (Lofty) Blomfield, founder of the Whangarei branch, in his heyday as the British Empire professional wrestling champion. IHC LIBRARY COLLECTION

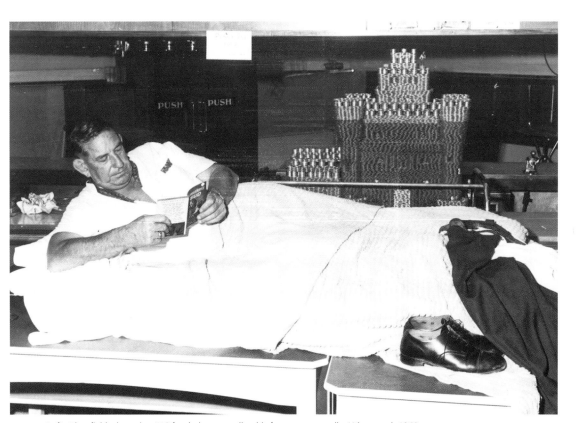

Lofty Blomfield, champion IHC fundraiser, guarding his famous penny pile, Whangarei, 1963. NORTHERN PUBLISHING

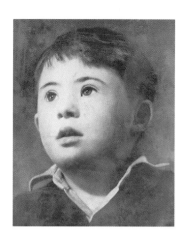

'Tony', the face of the IHC annual appeal, 1968.   IHC LIBRARY COLLECTION

Children of the South Taranaki branch after an outing.   HAWERA STAR PUBLISHING

Kew Home, Dunedin, 1971.   OTAGO DAILY TIMES

1972

Making toys and baskets, South Canterbury branch, 1972.

whom he negotiated ... During his long service he has been ably supported by Mrs Botting whose attendance at all IHC conferences has become an institution. Her kindly sympathy and support must have been an inspiration to our President. They were indeed an IHC team in themselves.

Although he retired from presidency, Stan Botting remained on the New Zealand Committee representing the Otago region.

And a New President

The new president, Dr D.M.G. (Donald) Beasley, then aged 44 was not only deeply committed to people with an intellectual disability but had a high profile in New Zealand medical circles and a developing relationship with representatives of allied organisations overseas. Two years later, when Dr Beasley was elected to the Council of the International League of Societies for the Mentally Handicapped, it was seen by New Zealand members as a great honour.

The operating costs of the IHCS had grown to such an extent that despite subsidies, legacies and donations, branch committees and members were facing huge financial commitments. Fundraising, which at best required optimism, enthusiasm and initiative, threatened to become an overwhelming burden. Nevertheless the society continued to expand its services. By 1967 its 28 branches had established 14 day-care centres for 170 children; four pre-school centres for 44 children; 10 occupational groups with a total roll of 96; 22 occupational centres with a total roll of 431 adults. The IHCS had registered a total of 2545 people with intellectual disability.

Dr Beasley and the New Zealand Committee constantly expressed the worry that voluntary donations from the public and government subsidies would not suffice. Within two years the government had granted 50 per cent salary subsidies for approved day-care centre staff and branch administrators, and raised from $1.20 to $1.60 per resident per night the running-cost subsidy for children under 16 years in IHCS hostels. The salary subsidies marked a commitment by the government to the society's work. It was with a sense of achievement that members approached the society's 'coming of age'.

Whither or Wither the Institutions?

An ongoing issue that generated much heat in the society was that of institu-tionalisation. Throughout the 1960s the Department of Health continued with its policy that the best way to help those with an intellectual disability was to improve and expand the institutions and to discourage families from keeping such children at home. The number of places in hospital institutions had increased from 550 in 1952 to more than 2000 by 1969. The Mental Health Act passed that year transferred control of psychiatric and psychopaedic hospitals from the Mental Hygiene Division to local hospital boards and changed the procedures for admission to and discharge from such institutions. As a result more people became voluntary and short-term patients.

Parents' attitudes towards institutions differed according to their circum-stances. The Reverend Pat Gourdie, vicar of Shannon, shared his views on institutions (as father of a Down's Syndrome daughter) with other members in the society's journal.

> A very big question and a debatable one is 'What is best for the child?' Do the parents take him into their own home or do they place him in a special home for such children? We are in no doubt that each case must be treated on its own merits, no rule-of-thumb procedure can be laid down and all relevant matters must be taken into consideration.

The writer's daughter Janet remained at home with her parents and four siblings until her death at age 11. 'She was indeed a blessing to a great number of people and to us her parents, brother and sisters in particular.'

A response from another member, published in the next issue of the journal, while it was sympathetic to and appreciative of the case of little Janet, put forward a different viewpoint.

> What of the children who don't die, and what of the effect on their parents and the rest of the family? We have more than one case in this town where the handicapped child is about 17 and the parents are most pitifully and prematurely aged and broken – the family life may have been kind and infinitely patient but it must have been unnatural. Our own handicapped child was born in 1937, the eldest of a family of four. He was not a Mongol but he never learned to walk steadily or to talk. In those days there were no schools for such children but we were visited and helped by ... the Crippled Children's Society and the Correspondence School. For 18 months we attended a speech clinic in the Hutt until I realised that Mark was making

no progress and was keeping a place from some child who would make better use of it.

By this time Mark was nearly 11 and I had two younger boys and a little girl. [They] all played happily and lovingly together, but the second boy began to feel a little shy about bringing his friends home and Mark himself was sometimes waylaid and teased when he went with a pushcart to do simple messages for me. His tears and bewilderment that anyone would hurt him used to hurt me more than I can say. I went to a lecture in Wellington by Dr Lennane. His advice was: 'If your child will never unaided be able to earn his own living he should go to an institution before he reaches his teens.' The decision was hard to make and harder still to carry out. We took Mark to the Levin Hospital and Training School when he was 11 and I can honestly say that we have never regretted it. I lost my husband by illness four years ago. My own health, both nervous and physical, was I am sure impaired by the strain of those early years. Mark is now 24. He greets us with joy when we visit him which we do as often as we can. I am so glad from the bottom of my heart to feel that he is safe and will be cared for tenderly whatever happens to me and that he will not be an embarrassment or a burden to his brothers or sister.

Official policy of the society on the matter of institutions in the latter 1960s was somewhat ambivalent. Under the heading 'Psychopaedic Hospitals' an IHCS information sheet stated:

> Although the trend is more and more to community participation and acceptance, the psychopaedic hospital has a fundamental and essential responsibility – to provide skilled staff, trained in all aspects of the care of the intellectually handicapped; to provide basic nursing for the most severely handicapped; to provide skilled psychiatric care for the disturbed intellectually handicapped; to provide skilled diagnosis and to provide appropriate training and sheltered workshop employment for those who for one reason or another cannot be placed in the community.

Institutions in the meantime continued to grow. Murray Priest, born in 1942, was one who after years of fostering and working for people had experience of institutional life in the 1960s.

> At 21, the Welfare people stopped looking after me. I suppose I had nowhere else to go, so I was given a choice of hospital in Wellington or Nelson. I didn't know what they were talking about and thought I must have been sick. When I got to Ngawhatu [Nelson] it was a bit of a shock. I was there for ten years when I met a friend who worked there and everything started to change slowly. There was a light at the end of the tunnel. I started to go out for weekends

and met other friends. Then the medical superintendent was very pleased for me to go out and board with a family. From then on after boarding here and there and working in a racing stable for a couple of years, then doing housework and baby-sitting, I joined IHC [Nelson branch] and I have gone from strength to strength and proved my capabilities.

Charlie Waigth remembers when his daughter Catherine was admitted to the newly opened Mangere Hospital in the mid-1970s. It had been a difficult decision to put her there, but at the time his wife was not well and it seemed the only place suitable to cope with Catherine's hyperactivity and habit of running away, as well as her other needs. Catherine came home every second weekend, but even so took two years to settle at Mangere, where she remained for a total of six years.

4

A Vision Becomes Reality

Coming of Age: 1970s

The under-secretary to the Minister of Education opened the 1970 annual conference of the IHCS in Blenheim on a positive note:

> The story of the Society's rise from small beginnings to the large and vital national organisation of today is in many respects a masterpiece of public relations by voluntary and dedicated citizens convinced of their cause and so enthusiastic that they successfully carried this enthusiasm to gain the co-operation of the whole community.

The Society was celebrating its 21st anniversary: a time to look back as well as forward. Some of the old pioneers had gone. Harold S. Anyon had died at his home in Waikanae in March 1965. The Bottings had retired from active membership. Both were now life members and at the 21st birthday function, held at the conference, had the honour of cutting the cake. Mary Botting died the following year but Stan Botting lived to the great old age of 99, dying in 1991.

The relationship between the Anyons and the New Zealand Committee of the society was still somewhat strained but their far-sighted pioneering work was acknowledged at this time. At its AGM the Wellington branch paid tribute to the founders and Margaret Anyon was pictured cutting the 21st birthday cake. Jean Clark, the branch president, recalled the tremendous efforts of the Anyons in the formation of the IHCPA in 1949 and read extracts from early submissions to the government.

> It is of interest to note that in these early submissions there was reference to the need for pre-schooling, schooling, occupation for adults, residential homes, child health clinics, speech therapy, hospital visiting committees, medical and dental care and a register to reveal the incidence of intellectual handicap – all services which we have since obtained or still require.

Margaret Anyon's life continued to revolve around her son Keith, an obsession that was sometimes the cause of friction within the family. The Anyon parents had always been aware and concerned that Keith would outlive them and, like all parents, worried about who would care for him when they had died. After they left the Wellington branch, they had joined forces with Hal Anyon's old friend Lew Harris and helped Hawke's Bay members to establish Hohepa, the new hostel with other facilities in Clive. The plan was formulated that with Mrs Anyon widowed and elderly and finding it more difficult to care for Keith at home, he could move into this new hostel.

So it was that a few years after Hal Anyon's death, Peter Anyon took a weekend off from his busy medical practice to drive his mother and brother to Hawke's Bay: a long trip in a Ford Prefect. Peter later recalled that when they arrived the Anyons booked into a Te Mata motel for the night. Next day they settled Keith into the hostel, and Peter drove his mother back to Wellington. A week later the Anyons had a phone call from Hohepa. Keith was unsuitable for the hostel: he was too old, very wilful and independent and created management problems. Peter drove all the way back up to Hawke's Bay to collect his brother and bring him back to Wellington.

Another pioneer and popular high-profile member passed on. It was a shock for members to hear that M.S. ('Lofty') Blomfield, famous for his gold-toothed smile, had died suddenly in June 1971 aged 63. Acknowledged as a founder of the Northland branch he had served on the New Zealand Committee since 1953. Tributes flowed in for Lofty, who had been a great worker and fundraiser for the IHC. Said Dr Beasley:

> Mr M.S. (Lofty) Blomfield probably did more than anyone else has to convey the plight of the intellectually handicapped to the man in the street ... It was

really quite amazing that a man who was a physical hero and a superb athlete should have devoted so much of his life to this work.

J.D. Burn-Murdoch resigned from his official position in the society in 1973 after a long stint of service. He had been an early president of the South Auckland branch in Hamilton and from 1965 a member of the New Zealand Committee. In 1964 Jack and Hilda Burn-Murdoch and their son John moved to Tauranga where Jack worked with the Tauranga–Te Puke Branch. He was vice president of the society from 1966 and was largely responsible for planning and organisation of the National Appeal. Jack died in 1989.

Living on the Knife Edge

Money was always an issue: government subsidies came, but were always too little, too late. Dr Terry Caseley remembers his first New Zealand Committee meetings. 'We were discussing the budget which I think was like half a million dollars and wondering if we'd ever make it. We always seemed to be living on the knife edge, as it were, of financial difficulties.'

Through the continuous efforts of branch members and the co-ordinating efforts of the New Zealand Committee the IHC was constantly fundraising, pressing for subsidies, organising a building fund, and sharing resources for services. Those involved in the massive amount of work required for fundraising were encouraged by the knowledge that at the same time they were increasing public awareness and goodwill for the cause. Money came from the Golden Kiwi lottery funds, government subsidies and from various charities, notably the Sutherland Trust. IHC representatives made regular submissions to the Minister of Internal Affairs for a more substantial grant from the Golden Kiwi: the society in 1964 was receiving £15,000, which was only 1.5 per cent of all welfare grants made by the Golden Kiwi.

While the branches continued with their raffles and other more innovative fundraising activities, a scheme promulgated from the national office in 1964 and organised through the branches involved the issue of key tags at motor vehicle re-licensing time in June of each year. The scheme was sponsored by Caltex Oil (NZ) and in 1970 the society reported that in the six years since its inception 'more than 15,000 motorists whose keys have been lost have been helped out of some difficult situations and the Society has benefited from donations totalling $50,000. An average of about 50 [lost] keys pour into the Society's Post Office box in Wellington every week. The owners are traced and the keys returned to them.'

The national appeal was 'dreamed up' in 1966, the year before the advent of decimal currency. O.I. 'Ossie' Jones remembers how it began.

> At a special meeting of the North Shore executive, fundraising was discussed. I pointed out that there were two major house-to-house appeals in existence already and that six other organisations were thinking of starting up theirs. I felt IHC should initiate an appeal promptly and become the third established appeal in New Zealand.

His remit was passed at the next national conference and planning began. 'IHC advertised for a person to initiate the appeal, but all the advertising failed as the entrepreneurs available and competent to do the job had dollar signs in their eyes.'

The New Zealand Committee appointed an appeal sub-committee and sent Stan King up to the North Shore branch to persuade Ossie Jones to work for the society. Ossie left his business in his wife's capable hands and for £3500 per annum became the first IHC appeal director.

> We scheduled the appeal for 12 months on, but to test the water first we held a mini appeal in Southland. The £8000 we raised encouraged us to proceed. Then followed for us tedious months of mapping the country ... visits to every town and city in New Zealand, meeting with local committees, women's institutes, service clubs.

Another member recalls:

> We received a notice in Hamilton to discuss the thing. No one knew what it was all about. I was suspicious and felt that whatever it was, it might be demanding of us and so I was delighted when someone else volunteered to go. Unfortunately the volunteer never got there so we never received the warnings about what had to be done.

The first house-to-house appeal was conducted in April 1967.

> Suddenly the national appeal was on us. There were no plans, no maps or contacts, we had to cover the counties of Hauraki Plains, Thames and Coromandel as well as the towns of Thames and Paeroa ... Every night for two weeks I rang every available organisation in every town of the whole area.

I will always have great respect for the women's organisations – the Women's Division of Federated Farmers, the Country Women's Institute. They hardly ever failed me and if they couldn't assist they suggested people who could. Sometimes I had to make several rings from their suggestions but I always found someone who would help. I got the Scouts in one town and in another, when I was desperate, the local RSA stepped into the breach. Service clubs were organised in Paeroa and the sub-branch committee helped the service clubs in Thames.

The first national appeal took most of the day but the yield made it all worth while. 'We thought that all our troubles stemming from a lack of finances were going to be over. We are always optimistic, aren't we?' The job of national appeal chairman was taken over first by J.D. Burn-Murdoch and its aims were high. Dr Beasley pointed out in 1968: 'At present the Society must raise $200,000 a year to meet running costs, and its capital budget over the next three years to meet urgently needed extensions exceeds $1,800,000.' In that year the appeal raised $303,000, with $279,000 in 1969 and $356,000 in 1970.

J.B. Brotherston took over as chair of the National Appeal Committee in 1974 and the following year the IHC national appeal became part of IHC Week. Publicity emphasised the needs of the intellectually handicapped in the community and the proceeds from the national appeal for the first time topped half a million dollars. In 1977 Telethon raised a huge $2 million for mental health, of which the society received a portion.

Personal Advocacy Trust

The annual conference in Hastings in 1965 approved the establishment of a trusteeship scheme which was launched in 1968. The idea was to ensure that people with sympathy and understanding would be appointed to watch over the interests and welfare of people with an intellectual disability after the death of their parents. Children could be registered through the provision by the parents of a legacy, a gift or an insurance policy cover of $1000, which would become available to the trust on the death of the parents. In 1972 the trusteeship scheme had 120 registrations and within five years registrations numbered 350.

By the 1980s the scheme had been named the Personal Advocacy Trust and was operating as a wide network all over New Zealand, with district advisers co-ordinating the programme. One woman who answered an advertisement for advocates was a retired teacher. She remembers that as an advocate she was allocated a client and expected to visit and report on the client's welfare at least once per month (most do more). She was paid $10 an hour, plus expenses. When she herself later became a district adviser, she was better paid but had considerably more responsibility. She became the 'next of kin' for two clients who had no relatives still living. When one of the clients died unexpectedly she had to arrange his funeral, which she found a big responsibility. 'I had to decide where to hold it, what sort of coffin he should have and whether he should be cremated. We had the funeral at the chapel in Porirua Hospital.'

Parents or guardians who paid money into the trust sometimes left specific requests concerning their children. One family whose son loved to go on outings to McDonald's left money so that he could be taken by taxi on a weekly trip to the restaurant. Another man said that he and his son always made a special trip to watch the 21-gun salute on Queen's Birthday weekend. He left money and instructions that every year at Queen's Birthday his son was to be dressed up for the occasion and taken to watch the ceremony.

The longest-running debate at the 1964 conference was over a remit recommending the appointment of a full-time organiser for the society. Although it was heavily defeated, the issue surfaced again and again in the next few years. As the society grew, the burden of administration and handling the financial matters became increasingly heavy. There was a perceived need to become more professional and formal, and a legal requirement to be accountable to members, their 'children' and to the general public and the government for use of public money. This latter was particularly relevant as the IHC had become one of the largest and most active voluntary agencies in New Zealand.

In 1968 the IHC appointed three paid branch managers: Mrs Maureen Tilly (South Auckland), Don Hodder (North Shore) and JB Munro (Southland). The following year Auckland's first branch administrator, R. Sanford, was appointed. That year in the national office in Wellington, what Dr Beasley regarded as a most important decision was finally made to appoint national advisers. D.J. (Doug) Callander became adviser on services, to take some of the workload off the shoulders of general secretary R.G. Mathews. He was followed by Dorothy Howie, and in 1979, Angus Capie. In 1973 as well as a general secretary the society appointed a national executive officer: Air Commodore E.W. Tacon. Napier born, Bill Tacon had had a long and distinguished career in the air force and was married with six children. As well as general administration at national office, mainly concerned with the national appeal, his task was to liaise with and assist the branches.

Books and Other Resources

In the 1940s when Margaret Anyon had looked for information about her son's condition she could not find a single book on the subject in any New Zealand library. For parents with disabled children Pearl Buck's *The Child Who Never Grew*, published in 1951, was a tremendous boost for the morale. Subsequently the Country Library Service established special collections covering topics such as disabilities.

Years later, in 1967, the IHCS head office in Wellington established a library, set up by Mrs M. Walmsley with 52 books. So popular was this service that, largely thanks to the hard work of the new librarian, Mrs D. Skinner, within three years the library reported that 240 books and 34 journals had been added to the library and 364 books had been borrowed. A catalogue of library books available for borrowing by post was available in each of the IHC branches. By the 1990s under Liz MacGibbon the IHC library had joined the nationwide library computer network.

In 1969 the society's journal reported that the National Film Library in Wellington had 20 films dealing with aspects of intellectual handicap available for loan to branches all over New Zealand. The IHC library also added films to its growing collection. One of these films was New Zealand made and featured the work of the IHC's Gisborne Branch. Called *A Place in Society*, filmed by D. Walker in 1968, it won the Federation of New Zealand Amateur Cinema Society's annual competition. Another documentary, *Thursday's Child*, made by the National Film Unit, was shown on New Zealand television in February 1972 and the docu/drama *You Can't Manage on Your Own*, produced for the IHCS, was also screened on nationwide television, in February 1974.

Other resources became available. In great demand was a recording and accompanying booklet produced by the Radio New Zealand Continuing Education Unit based on a series of seven radio talks: *Your Child is Different*.

Research: Surveys and Findings

In 1969 the society set up a sub-committee for research into intellectual handicap, from which a board of trustees made funds available for research projects. Encouraged by Dr Beasley, the New Zealand Committee members understood the need for proper and comprehensive information about the prevalence, types of disorder and depth of intellectual handicap occurring in New Zealand. The society was continually requesting from the Department of Education and its own branches and other agencies notification of the occurrence of intellectual handicap but there was still no overall statistical register on the incidence of intellectual disability.

Meanwhile, the New Zealand Department of Health published in 1972 E.H. Densem's *Persons with Mental Retardation in Wellington and Northland: A Report on an Accommodation Survey*. The intention was to enumerate all children and adults in the region with an IQ below 85 who had a 'clinical need' or 'social, physical or psychological factors which require the facilities and training generally reserved for mentally retarded persons'. By this definition the author identified 2860 retarded persons in the area of study and calculated an overall prevalence rate of 3.71.

The aims of the IHCS Survey undertaken by A.A. Morrison, Dr Beasley and K.I. Williamson and published in 1976, were even more ambitious and comprehensive. They aimed to

> ascertain the prevalence of intellectual handicap in New Zealand; secondly to record in broad terms the physical characteristics, degree of independence and self care and the patterns of behaviour identified as judged by the family; thirdly to record the composition of the family and the features of the family environment and the effect as perceived by the family of the presence of an intellectually handicapped person; and fourthly to record the need for services and facilities for the intellectually handicapped as perceived by the family.

The survey organisers selected five regions: three from the North Island and two from the South Island with a combined population of 728,896 aged 0–64 years, comprising 27.83 per cent of the total population in that age group as at 1971. Using these large samples of the population the survey designed quantitative questions to ascertain 'how many, how old, what sex, what race, what numbers were cared for at home, in hostels of various sorts, in hospitals and whether there were any unusual national, regional, geographic, socio-economic or other differences'. Qualitative questions addressed such matters as 'how retarded, how handicapped and whether additionally handicapped with physical, sensory, motor or behavioural disorders'.

A sample of 2396 people with an intellectual disability was identified and traced. One of the most important findings was establishing the incidence of a number of the major disorders defined by the WHO as known to be associated with children and adults with intellectual handicap:

Recognisable Handicapping Conditions and Associated Physical Disorders of the Intellectually Handicapped*

Disorder	Total No.	Total %
None	711	31.78
Epilepsy	469	20.97
Mongolism (Down's Syndrome)	438	19.58
Cerebral Palsy	313	13.99
Musculo/Skeletal	270	12.07
Respiratory	188	8.40
Cardiovascular	148	6.62
Obesity	114	5.10
Congenital Cranial Anomalies	97	4.34
Endocrinological	78	3.49
Alimentary	76	3.40
Minor Chronic Infections	75	3.35
Skin	56	2.50
Other Disorders of the Central Nervous System	50	2.24

*Percentages exceed 100, as two or more disorders were reported for some subjects.

Notable was the high correlation of physical and mental handicap.

The publication of the findings of this comprehensive survey of people with an intellectual disability in New Zealand, was a milestone not only in the history of the society but also in medical science. By late 1976 the New Zealand Committee was convinced of the need to have an independent body to address the issue of further research. The annual conference that year approved the establishment of a separate Scientific Council and Research Foundation. R.A. (later Sir Roy) McKenzie was elected chairman of the newly formed New Zealand Institute of Mental Retardation, which was incorporated as a separate entity to undertake and initiate research. The term mental retardation rather than intellectual handicap was chosen to emphasise that the focus of the institute would be mental retardation in its broad sense. Other members of the institute's trust board were: Mr J. Sutherland, R.G. Mathews (trustee and secretary), K.I. Williamson (former president of the Manawatu branch, now representing the president of the NZSIH) and Dr D.M.G. Beasley (director and trustee).

Support Organisations

Down's Syndrome Association

Of the conditions identified among IHC 'client' members, what is now known as Down's Syndrome was prevalent. The 1976 report recorded that 'Mongolism is the largest single identifiable condition which is accompanied by mental retardation'.

During the 1960s members debated at various times use of the term Mongol. At the 1965 annual conference in Hastings a move to have the term 'Mongol Child' replaced by 'Down's Syndrome Child' was defeated. Mongol was still in official use by the society in the 1970s, but the term Down's Syndrome was gradually accepted as new publications from overseas adopted the term.

In 1980 a group of mothers began getting together on a regular basis, organised by a social worker at Mangere Hospital. They had one thing in common: a baby with Down's Syndrome. Ngaire Garland remembers:

> As we got to know each other and to find out more about Down's Syndrome it became apparent that there were many things we began to think of as important or essential for the health and welfare of our babies, our families and ourselves, that were unavailable. Because none of us had anything much to do with disability the more we discovered about the current situation the more shocked and distressed we became.

A teacher, Ngaire had assumed that every child in New Zealand had an automatic right to go to school, and was appalled to learn that this was not the case for children with intellectual disabilities.

Parents of what had started as an informal group were encouraged to form a Down's Association. They began holding monthly meetings in Auckland and issued a monthly newsletter. By the end of 1982 the Down's Association under the IHC umbrella was well established and with financial assistance from IHC published a pamphlet about Down's Syndrome and prepared displays of photographs for exhibition in public places. Seven years later the association had eight branches and was sending out just under 600 monthly newsletters.

Autistic Association

Other disabling conditions were gradually being identified. In 1958 Marion Bruce gave birth to her fourth child, Andrew, in Patea where her husband Lyall had his medical practice. It was not until Andrew was about 18 months old that his parents became worried about his development. 'He didn't speak and he walked on his toes, he giggled a lot and he had very restricted preferences for food. We didn't know enough to put it together.' Although Marion wanted to seek advice, her husband was reluctant. 'What would we say?' he said. In any case they were living at quite a distance from paediatric specialists. When the Bruce family moved south to Porirua they approached a neurologist at Victoria University. He suggested that there was nothing wrong with their child and that if the Bruce parents could 'sort themselves out' all would be well. This was found to be a common attitude of medical professionals to developmental abnormalities at that period.

For Marion the crisis point came when Andrew approached school age and it appeared he could still not talk. She and Andrew found their way to the Psychological Services of the Education Department and for the first time heard the word 'autism'. Marion looked for books – without success – at the Porirua Hospital library, until the superintendent said to her: 'You don't want books, you want to go to the Child Health Clinic.' The clinic, within the Health Department, had a multi-disciplinary team who worked to assess children. 'They were marvellous,' recalls Marion. 'They said, "It's not your fault, it's nothing you've done."' This was a great relief to Marion and her husband, but the experts still had no specific suggestions as to treatment.

All the while Marion sought answers, Andrew was growing up without education. 'The local school refused to admit him as he could not speak, the deaf school would not take him as he was not deaf and the IHC had an occupational centre but said he was too bright.' Finally the Education Department agreed to fund a school in conjunction with the IHC, provided there was a minimum of 12 children. Although different from the others Andrew was accepted as number 11 and eventually Kapi Mana School came into being in the grounds of Cannons Creek School.

Meanwhile in 1966 Dr Mildred Creek, a world expert on autism, visited New Zealand and gave new hope to parents. Marion arranged for her to assess Andrew, then aged eight. 'She confirmed the diagnosis and gave two pieces of advice: broaden his diet and approach a Rudolf Steiner school.' The dietary advice was put into practice but having inspected a Steiner type of school in Hawke's Bay Marion was not persuaded of its suitability.

After Dr Creek's visit articles on autism began appearing in the IHC's journal. With encouragement from her husband Marion began actively seeking other parents with an autistic child and had soon organised a group of 19 families. She was well suited to this organisational role since before her marriage she had worked as a welfare and youth activities officer for the YWCA.

The extent of interest in autism became visible when 120 people attended a seminar on the autistic child organised by the Extension Department of Victoria University of Wellington.

Most parents contacted by Marion Bruce were already in touch with the IHC. In consultation, the parents decided to approach the society for support. In 1969 the IHC set up an autistic sub-committee, later known as the Autistic Association, chaired by Dr Terry Caseley with Margaret Stewart as secretary, both from Christchurch. A branch structure was also set up for the four main centres, with a representative from each branch on the national committee.

The Auckland branch with Bob Burnes as chairman and Philippa Stevens as secretary, was particularly active in the early 1970s, and soon established a unit for autistic children.

A national meeting in 1975 proved to be a turning point when the Dunedin branch of the Autistic Association wanted the association to break away from IHC and form its own incorporated society. The motion was defeated when the new director of the society, Bill Tacon, encouraged the Autistic Association instead to make greater use of the IHC. He pointed out that some branches had been raising funds to pay special teachers without realising that the society could help. There was also a feeling that New Zealand was too small for an independent organisation to become viable. But from that time the national director of the Autistic Association regularly attended national IHC committee meetings and the association was represented at New Zealand Committee meetings, annual conferences and in the annual report.

The Auckland branch of the Autistic Association ran a lot of seminars and courses, as did the branch in Christchurch. The Autistic Unit at Sylvia Park, Auckland, was formally taken over by the Department of Education in 1986.

Committee members at the twenty-first annual conference, Blenheim 1970.   IHC LIBRARY COLLECTION

Opening of conference, International League of Societies for the Mentally Handicapped, Wellington, 1974.
Dr Donald Beasley (right) was national president IHC 1964–79; president International League of Societies for
Persons with Mental Handicap, Brussels, 1974–78.   SOUTH PACIFIC PHOTOS LTD

Children at Redwoodtown School, Blenheim, fundraising for IHC, 1971. MARLBOROUGH EXPRESS

H.J. Walker, Minister of
Social Welfare 1975–78,
at Campbell House, Porirua
City. IHC LIBRARY COLLECTION

New Zealand Committee, annual conference 1978, Nelson. R.LUCAS & SON/NELSON EVENING MAIL

Dr Donald Beasley with Paul Heyes, who inspired the design of the IHC logo.

Mathews House, Dunedin: home of The Donald Beasley Institute. The building was named after Ray Mathews, general secretary IHC 1954–77. THE DONALD BEASLEY INSTITUTE

Ray Mathews, general secretary IHC (right), and his successor, JB Munro, annual conference 1978, Nelson.

Dr R.T.M. Caseley, national president IHC
1979–88.

IHC farm, Carrington Road, New Plymouth, 1979.   TARANAKI NEWSPAPERS LTD

J.P. (Mick) Murphy, chairman, Appeal
and Fundraising Sub-Committee,
1981–82.   IHC LIBRARY COLLECTION

Botting, first prize in the horse lottery 1983, making overtures to IHC patron Colin Meads, King Country. NZ HERALD

Richard Belton became president of the national committee of the Autistic Association in the late 1980s. By that period much more was known about the condition of autism and research increasingly came to be focused on the syndrome known as Asperger. In this type of autism the autistic child has no significant delays in language development and is often very articulate. Parents with autistic children now have the advantage of early diagnosis, skilled therapy and special educational help.

The Lost Girls: The Rett Syndrome

Kristen was born in 1968, the much wanted and loved 'magical' first child of Dr Roderick and Gillian Deane. All went well until Kristen was about 18 months old, when Gillian became concerned. Kristen's general health was poor, she had had a lot of ear infections, and developmentally had begun to regress. 'She stopped using words she had been using; she walked, but started screaming at nights.' Gillian consulted medical professionals: at least one was convinced that Kristen was autistic, another said he thought her condition was more complicated. Gillian read everything she could find in the hospital library and while she learned nothing more about Kristen's condition, she learned 'how to live without a diagnosis'. But she never gave up hope that one day she would find out.

Everywhere she went she looked for help with her daughter's condition. In 1974 the Deanes were travelling to the United States and while in the plane Kristen began to have seizures. On arrival Gillian had her daughter admitted to hospital where she was given a number of tests. 'She had all the tests except a brain biopsy. We refused to let them in case it did her harm.' The doctors in America were very supportive and fascinated by Kristen's condition but still had no diagnosis to offer the Deanes. Furthermore, they were concerned that Kristen's nervous system was degenerating and predicted that she would not live past the age of 10.

Back in New Zealand Gillian watched over her daughter night and day and did everything she could to keep her mobile and stimulated: walks, outings, music. They had already tried to obtain education for Kristen but her condition was so rare that she didn't fit in anywhere. Even IHC couldn't cope with the amount of individual care needed. 'She went to a school at Levin, but wasn't making any progress. They said they'd "special" her for a month on a one-to-one basis. After that we'd done everything that was ever suggested.'

The long-awaited diagnosis finally arrived at the very end of 1983 when Kristen was 15. 'A letter came from a paediatrician – a woman – in the United States that we had kept in contact with since the time we'd lived there.' The doctor wrote that she had been to hear a lecture from a French researcher and at the end had said: 'I've got one of those girls in New Zealand.' The letter included a list of all the symptoms of so-called Rett Syndrome. For Gillian it was a revelation, 'an amazing letter. Horrific, but so nice to know that there was nothing you could have done. It was all there.' She tried to telephone her husband but Roderick was not in his office, so bursting to tell someone, Gillian ran across the road to tell her GP. 'Once I got the diagnosis I felt a huge weight had gone from my shoulders; I could get on with my life.'

The information from the United States included the fact that Rett Syndrome affects only girls and that its incidence in the general population is very small. At the time of Kristen's diagnosis it was thought she might be the only one in New Zealand or even Australasia.

Roderick Deane was already involved with IHC and the society's president, Dr Terry Caseley, was very interested to hear the news about Rett Syndrome. JB Munro wanted the Deanes to take part in publicity, but they felt it would be an invasion of their privacy, although later a carefully worded article appeared in the *Sunday Star-Times*. Gillian also designed a bookmark to send to medical practitioners. With Dr Caseley's willing co-operation during the next few years, through the joint efforts of medical professionals and the parents of Rett girls, the society made contact with many families and was able to provide information and practical help.

According to statistical calculations it was estimated that there would be 25–30 girls in New Zealand with Rett Syndrome. By 1988 the association had discovered 12 such girls and within a year Gillian Deane, who became convenor of the Rett Association, reported that the register included 28 girls. At first the Deanes had felt incredible benefits from being in touch with the families of other Rett girls, but gradually came to realise that as well as the newsletter, which played an educational role, people needed to have local support and the sort of network provided by IHC branches. 'It was wonderful to see Rett girls in a classroom with other children,' she recalls. When Kristen died at age 27 Gillian wanted to give up her work with the Rett Syndrome Association but was persuaded to carry on.

Other Groups

Other affiliated groups were formed over the years, including in 1989 a national Prader-Willi Syndrome Association for parents and caregivers, with Mrs Linda Thornton as national secretary.

Into the Pacific

In the late 1960s New Zealand became more aware of its responsibilities towards the Pacific Islands. In 1968 the IHC resolved that efforts be made to arouse interest in the needs of people with an intellectual disability and promote the establishment of services in the Pacific, beginning with Fiji. The campaign began with writing letters directly to professionals and prominent citizens in Fiji, to church workers and to service clubs as well as directly to parents of children with intellectual disability. There was little response until the *Suva Times* published articles from New Zealand on intellectual disability. At that point Fiji Jaycees expressed interest and their national vice-president visited New Zealand as a guest of the IHC. Not long afterwards Dr Donald Beasley and Lofty Blomfield, who both had friends and fans in the Islands, visited Fiji. They had an audience with the Prime Minister and appointments with Ministers of the Crown, heads of government departments and local body officials. As well they met with medical and educational colleagues of Dr Beasley, social workers, church groups and service clubs.

As a result of this visit, and a second trip made by Dr Beasley and Ray Mathews, the New Zealanders gradually came to understand the needs of the Pacific Island people in the matter of the intellectually handicapped. The Islands had extended family networks rather than sophisticated organisations. They needed support and understanding, as well as reassurance in some cases that disability was not a curse sent by God. Within a few years of the New Zealanders' first visits a society for the mentally handicapped was established in Fiji and services gradually developed. Pre-schools came first, and later schools and workshops, with educational authorities assuming responsibility for financial assistance in training staff. New Zealand IHC representatives made sporadic visits to Fiji, and Lofty Blomfield was sadly missed after his death by all his friends there.

An effort was also made to promote interest in the work of the IHC in Tonga, largely through the efforts of Laureen Munro, an expatriate New Zealand woman with a daughter with an intellectual disability. In 1975 the Red Cross Society set up a small day-care facility in Tonga. Later support came rapidly with acceptance of the movement by the Tongan royal family. The King of Tonga opened the new centre for people with an intellectual disability in March 1979 and later that year the Queen of Tonga while in New Zealand visited IHC facilities in Southland. By 1993 when New Zealand representatives visited, Tonga had a school for children with an intellectual handicap, an adult workshop and hostel, a unit for hearing-impaired children and an outreach programme.

In 1978 the New Zealand IHC established the Asian and Pacific Action Committee, known as APAC, a special sub-committee to support services for people with intellectual disabilities in a dozen developing countries. Members included Laureen Munro (who became Laureen Outtrim), Mike Ryan, Don Wills, Keith Williamson, Alastair Lloyd, Dr Donald Beasley and Dr Terry Caseley. The original membership of APAC was soon to be strengthened by the addition of Gordon Palmer (Timaru IHC), Cliff Hemuli (Tonga), Jan Gough (Auckland IHC) and Beverley Robinson (Taranaki IHC), but was later reduced to four.

Auckland businessman Don Wills was one who stayed with the team. He and his wife Maureen had become involved in the IHC in the 1960s after their daughter Patricia was diagnosed as having an intellectual disability. Don was invited to a parent group meeting at a community centre which led to the formation of an Auckland sub-branch in Glen Innes. At first he was a committee member, then he took on more responsibility, liaised with the Auckland branch and in time became a regional representative on the New Zealand Committee. 'We met in a tiny room in Brandon House, Featherston Street, all squashed in, hardly room to breathe,' he recalled. One day in 1979 Graeme Reid, president of the Auckland branch, phoned and asked Don Wills to come around for a chat and over a bottle of Teachers suggested he become the next Auckland vice-president for the IHC. 'I took it on. The first AGM happened on the same night as we heard about the Erebus plane crash disaster. One guy there used to query our finances, he was an accountant with Air New Zealand. He went white when the news came of the missing plane.'

Meanwhile the pattern became established of bringing people from the Islands to New Zealand as guests of the society for orientation and training. Developments were already happening in Western Samoa after a visit in 1978 by

Dr Beasley. The Western Samoa IHC was born the following year, operating from a small building. Their new centre opened in 1985.

Annual visits were made to the Cook Islands by New Zealand representatives and the society for six years provided funding for an administrator. The Cook Islands Disabled Persons' Institute opened a new centre in 1983 and New Zealand supported a delegation in a bid to gain assistance from the Ministry of Education. Their efforts were rewarded and the disabled children in the Cook Islands gained access to schooling. In 1993 Don Wills was in Rarotonga for the opening of a week-long rehabilitation workshop for disability services on the outer islands.

In 1981 APAC contacted the newly formed Solomon Islands Handicapped Children's Centre in Honiara; Laureen Outtrim followed up with a visit. Help from New Zealand included salary support for the teachers plus equipment and training.

In the 1980s New Zealand's APAC renewed links with Fiji and funded Suva's IHC administrator and also a pottery unit. APAC had a special relationship with the Fiji Rehabilitation Council and sent resource staff to work with the council in Suva.

The New Zealand Red Cross linked APAC with Tuvalu Red Cross to help set up a home-based support service to disabled people and their families. APAC paid salaries for the two welfare field officers working out of Funafuti and covering the far-flung island groups. Laureen Outtrim, APAC's administration liaison officer, first visited Tuvalu and Niue in 1987. She found that Niuean people with disabilities were well cared for and integrated in their families and villages. APAC was able to provide help in the form of wheelchairs, a toy library and essential medical supplies.

First New Zealand contact with Vanuatu came in 1982 in response to a request from a parent of a disabled child who was attempting to establish a home-support programme in Port Vila. When Laureen visited she found the Red Cross was running a small centre operating one morning a week, attended by 20 disabled children and adults. Three years later Laureen visited and in conjunction with a steering committee brought into being a long-term plan to form a new organisation, the Handikap Sosaeti Blong Vanuatu. By 1989 the IHC had its own centre in Port Vila and was making moves towards employing full-time staff.

In 1991 APAC was replaced by the South Pacific Disability Council (SPDC), independent from but supported by the IHC New Zealand Committee.

Marking Time

'There is still no integrated scheme for the care and training of the intellectually handicapped in this country,' said Dr Beasley in his 1970 annual report. He rejected the idea that the society confine itself to persuading the government to take responsibility for the much-needed services. The society should continue to 'pioneer' some services and 'maintain' others. Overall the IHC should press the government to establish a comprehensive nationwide scheme serving all people with an intellectual disability by either providing such services or helping the society to do so. He saw IHC as a partner with the state in providing facilities for the intellectually handicapped. The society was assisting the government by harnessing public goodwill to aid the handicapped. Then came news from abroad that raised morale for all involved. The International League of Societies for the Mentally Handicapped in 1970 had adopted a Declaration of General and Special Rights of the Mentally Retarded. One of the rights expressed in its seven articles read: 'The mentally retarded person has the same basic rights as other citizens of the same country and same age.' Two years later the United Nations General Assembly adopted and published its Declaration on the Rights of Mentally Retarded Persons, which became the cornerstone of the society's philosophy.

The society made lengthy submissions to the 1971 Royal Commission on Social Security covering all matters concerning people with an intellectual disability, particularly stressing the need for co-ordination of services between the various government agencies and voluntary organisations: 'The intellectually handicapped are the largest dependent group in the community. The nature of this handicap has a most profound effect economically, socially and emotionally on the family and the community.' While deliberating, members of the royal commission visited IHC centres in the Wellington area to observe activities at first hand.

Four years later came the Royal Commission on Psychopaedic Hospitals. Although the notion of community care had been very much to the fore, the Ministry of Health set aside $5 million to further develop the big state-owned psychopaedic institutions. JB Munro, then an MP, was a member of the Health Committee, which later re-directed the money into the community via the hospital boards. He also, while in Parliament, negotiated with legislative draughtsmen to make a workable document and as a result the Disabled Persons' Community Welfare Bill had its first reading and was referred to the Social

Services Select Committee. Munro was not originally on this committee, but after some intensive lobbying and manoeuvring, he took the place of Ethel McMillan MP when she was sent to London. With three months to go before the end of the 1975 parliamentary year and, as it transpired, the Labour government's term in office, the committee under Dr Gerard Wall was making slow progress, and Munro was increasingly frustrated. Then fate took a hand. Dr Wall was hurt in a fall on the steps of Parliament and Munro was catapulted into the chair.

'We closed off the submissions and began to ready the bill.' When Prime Minister Bill Rowling asked caucus whether there was any outstanding legislation to go through, Munro mentioned the Disabled Persons' Community Welfare Bill. Rowling told Munro to get it in that day and he would see what he could do.

'We got the blue ribbon on it and it was introduced in the House that afternoon ... we finally got it through with about three days to spare.' JB Munro later stated that if the bill had not been passed then, before the National Party came to power, it might never have seen the light of day. Even then the struggle was not over and concerned MPs and watchdog bodies had to keep the pressure on, lobbying the various ministers and keeping civil servants up to date and informed, to ensure the legislation was passed into law.

The society also made submissions to the controversial 1977 Royal Commission of Enquiry into Contraception, Sterilisation and Abortion in New Zealand. But in the resultant act, as recorded by JB Munro, the position of the intellectually handicapped 'went from being less than ideal to disastrous'. The New Zealand Committee of the society was particularly concerned that the act failed to give clear direction or provide for substituted consent for a sterilisation operation on a child who could not give informed consent.

In 1974 the society celebrated its 25th anniversary. To mark the occasion the journal published a feature article on the pioneering work of Margaret Anyon, who observed that much progress had been made in the 25 years of the society's operation: 'I realise that our first demands were justified and many good hands and hearts have continued the work for its own sake.' The ongoing management of her son Keith, now in his late thirties, was still a matter of concern to the family. Keith's brother Peter and his wife regularly took Keith into their home in order to give their mother a break from day-to-day caring. Peter felt that his mother was becoming too old and frail to cope with Keith, yet when the crunch came, Margaret Anyon couldn't part with her younger son except for short periods. Peter thought the IHC should take more responsibility for Keith and there were frequent disagreements with the IHC. At one point Peter threatened to certify his brother. Eventually a suitable place was found for Keith at the Kristina Jepsen Senior Home at Silverstream, where he also had access to occupational activity and companionship at the Hutt Valley IHC workshop. He always went home to his mother for the weekend. Margaret Anyon died in 1976; Keith remained in the Jepsen home until his death in 1993.

At the funeral service for Keith Anyon, one of those who spoke on behalf of the IHC was JB Munro. Of the trail-blazing work of the Anyons he said: 'The fact is that it was Keith who was the cause. Had he not been born the history books could well be quite different. Of how many of us will that be said when our time comes? It was Keith Anyon whose life created a huge social revolution.'

The 1974 annual conference held in March in Wellington was timed to coincide with an important international event: the first South Pacific conference of the International League of Societies for the Mentally Handicapped. It was considered an honour to New Zealand when Dr Beasley was elected president of the ILSMH later that year.

At the 1975 conference hosted by the Buller–Westland branch in Greymouth, a significant development was another name change from the Intellectually Handicapped Children's Society to the New Zealand Society for the Intellectually Handicapped (NZSIH). It was a move that had been suggested at previous conferences, but resisted because the letters IHC had by that time achieved a great deal of public awareness and recognition. Those in favour of the change pointed out that two-thirds or more of the people now looked after by the society were over the age of 12 and it did little for the feelings and dignity of the adults to be referred to as children. President Dr Beasley considered it would be a 'progressive step if the name were changed'. The delegates voted 12 against, 43 in favour of the change. The next issue of the journal reflected the change when it became *Intellectual Handicap Review*, or *I.H. Review*. Name changes on stationery, brochures and signs were expected to be completed by 1 April 1976.

5

With JB in the Fast Lane

Into the Eighties

To face the new decade the NZSIH had a new President, Dr Richard Terence Maidstone Caseley, and a change of premises. National office in Wellington had moved in December 1979 out of its three little offices on the sixth floor of Brandon House in Featherston Street. The new premises, which had the advantage of a wheelchair ramp from the street, were on the fourth floor of the Gleneagles Building at 69–71 The Terrace.

Dr Terry Caseley was voted in at the 1979 annual conference in New Plymouth to take over as president from Dr Beasley who had held the office for 15 years. Dr Caseley was then in his forties and, like his predecessor, was not a parent of a child with an intellectual disability but a medical professional whose interest in the society derived from his work in paediatrics. He had worked in London in the early 1960s and in 1966 returned to the paediatrics department of Christchurch Hospital. It was his friend and predecessor Dr Beasley who persuaded him to become involved with IHC. Dr Beasley was in Christchurch to address a meeting of the local IHC branch, which at that time was not very strong because with Templeton Hospital being in Christchurch many parents had their needs met. As Terry Caseley recalls: 'I went to a meeting and I got up and said how important family was in terms of the child with the disability and then I was encouraged to take an interest in the local branch of the society.' Caseley was looking for a way to put something back into the community: 'I wanted to find something that would allow me to use the skills I'd developed.' Within just a few years he became president of the Christchurch branch working closely with secretary Maurice Le Febvre and his wife. Together they spearheaded a major fundraising campaign in the early 1970s to put up a day-care centre and two 10-bed hostels, in line with the thinking of the society at the time.

Dr Caseley shared the leadership of the NZSIH with two vice-presidents, Jack Brotherston (Wanganui) and J.G.S. Reid (Auckland). Ray Mathews was his 'brilliant' administrator. Terry Caseley recalls the 1970s well. 'There was also a passion in those days that people had. It was a great honour to be there to represent your branch at the New Zealand conference and people would put up remits and argue furiously about them. That was really interesting – how committed people were to the Society and how involved they were.'

Change came on the executive side when JB Munro, who had been Southland branch administrator 1968–1973, was appointed the society's first national executive director in 1977. IHC by then had an annual operating budget of about $8 million and the national office staff (including the librarian) numbered no more than five. Then aged 41, Munro was a former member of Parliament and Invercargill city councillor. He already had 20 years' involvement in community work and a lifetime of personal involvement with disability.

Born in Gore in 1936, John Baldwin Munro was only a few weeks old when he contracted polio, which was epidemic in that period. The disease affected his left leg and as a result he was unable to walk until the age of three: and then only with the aid of a calliper. Later he had a series of operations at Dunedin Hospital to straighten the leg but it was mainly through his own determination to play sport and live like other children that by age 16 he was able to discard the calliper permanently. While he was growing up JB had involvement with the Crippled Children's Society because of his own disability. He also had a half-brother who was confined to a wheelchair. In this way he gained first-hand experience with the problems of physical access for the handicapped – such as inaccessible toilets – and the advantages of ramps instead of steps. After leaving school JB worked for Vacuum Oil for three years, and then in 1958 started working for the YMCA, first in Invercargill and later in Dunedin, where he was general secretary for five years. He later remarked:

I didn't have a great deal of contact with intellectual disability until one day I noticed a young gentleman looking inside the door at a trampoline in the YMCA foyer. I went out and asked if he would like a bounce on it. It turned out he had Down's Syndrome and he introduced me to some of his friends out at the Kew Home in Caversham, later sold to IHC as its Dunedin headquarters ... After getting to know them I arranged for a group to come into the YMCA where I ran a physical education class for them ... my first one-on-one encounter with people with an intellectual handicap.

He little knew then that it was only the beginning and that it was David Botting, the son of Stan Botting, who was the young gentleman wanting a bounce on the trampoline.

JB and the Lion

In 1968 JB Munro began work for the IHC as administrator for the Southland branch and three years later was elected to the Invercargill City Council. One of his roles in IHC was fundraising and soon after he became a councillor a chance arose to not only gain publicity but to raise a good deal of money for the branch. A visiting circus asked permission of the council to stage a show on Sunday. The council agreed on condition that proceeds went to charity, and Munro was able to negotiate for the money to go to the IHC. As a special feature, wanting to attract a big crowd, he agreed to go into the ring to have a seesaw with a lion.

A lot of people were quite happy to see me gobbled up, so we filled the Big Top and made $1000 for IHC on the way. The money was put into my son's schoolbag, which was placed on the centre of the seesaw ... The beast was brought in. It sat on its end of the seesaw, then moved up towards the fulcrum so my end came down. I stood on my end and away we went, with the money slithering backwards and forwards between us as the crowd roared or gasped. Eventually I grabbed the satchel, jumped off and ran for my life.

It was after this stunt that JB Munro was asked by the Labour Party to stand as a candidate in the next election and duly became MP for Invercargill. But he never swerved from or forgot his allegiance to people with a disability and tried to get on every possible select committee that had anything to do with health or disability. In the run-up to the 1975 election the tide was turning against Labour. Ray Mathews rang JB and spelled out the obvious. 'You know you're not going to win.' Sure enough, within weeks JB Munro had lost his seat, but was offered work fundraising for the Labour Party with the idea that at the next election he would campaign to take back the Invercargill seat.

Events conspired otherwise. At Wellington Airport JB Munro happened to meet Donald Beasley, who said: 'Did you know that the society is looking for a national director?' JB was not especially interested in going back to Wellington but when he saw the advertisement in the newspaper he and his wife discussed the idea. Despite their reluctance to leave Invercargill JB put in an application for the job. 'The interview panel consisted of the entire New Zealand Committee of 16 people. The three women all voted against me, but I got the job and later became good friends with all three.' Donald Beasley has noted about the decision to appoint JB that 'some members of the committee were aghast' and that he had to talk pretty fast. 'But I said I do know … he has tremendous ideas and vision. I know what he's done in Invercargill. He's the sort of person you don't have to kick. You have to hang on to his coat-tails, he's so on the go.'

Constitutional Changes

Structurally from this time the society had two separate operations: paid administrative personnel headed by the national executive director, and a parallel branch structure of members and volunteers headed by the society's president. Also significant was a major change in the makeup of the New Zealand Committee. A regional system of representation had been introduced in 1965 but as time went on and the number of branches increased it seemed important to Dr Beasley, then president, to have all represented on the New Zealand Committee, the controlling body of the society. He was disappointed when in 1978 a proposal to this effect was turned down at the annual conference in Nelson. The change to full branch representation finally occurred a few years later at the 1981 annual conference in Blenheim. From that time the New Zealand Committee was made up of a national president and two vice-presidents elected at the conference, and the president (or a nominee) of each branch of the society. The value of the change the then President Dr Caseley suggested would be that branches would have a greater involvement in decision-making.

> The Executive Subcommittee would be answerable and accountable to New Zealand Committee ... because each Branch would be represented on NZ Committee it would improve the quality of communication and each Branch would have the opportunity to contribute ... It would inculcate a sense of family within the whole Society and a feeling of being in there together to serve the IH.

There were at that time 32 branches, which 10 years later had proliferated to 49. By then the Auckland branch had developed so many sub-branches that in 1985 it was decided to disincorporate the branch, which was ceremoniously achieved in the presence of Mayor Catherine (later Dame Catherine) Tizard. In its place the society created four separate full branches in the Auckland metropolitan area, which by the late 1980s had again multiplied with the growth of population.

'Carrying on': A New Generation of Parents

Despite the many advances and new services, parents of children with an intellectual disability faced many of the same difficulties as those of earlier generations.

In September 1977 after an uneventful pregnancy Lynne gave birth to her second baby boy. He was very small and jaundiced but otherwise neither Lynne nor her husband noticed anything unusual. Three months later, when Lynne took baby Duncan to the doctor for his second round of injections, came the bombshell.

'I have to tell you something. We've been putting it off until we thought you were ready. Your child has a genetic abnormality.'

Lynne spun her baby around and looked him full in the face.

'He's Down's, isn't he? Why didn't you tell me earlier?'

'We wanted to make sure you had bonded with him.'

'How long have you known?'

'We knew at the six-week check,' said the doctor, 'but we'll do a blood test to confirm the diagnosis.'

In fact, as Lynne discovered, the midwives at the hospital had known that Duncan was Down's Syndrome immediately after the birth.

What do I do? Lynne was thinking, and five minutes later she realised that she was automatically breast feeding her baby. That was the answer. 'I'll just carry on.' She went home, hung out the washing, and rang her husband at his work. 'He burst into tears and was terribly upset when I told him. In the end I had to go in and get him to come home.'

Lynne was already involved in the women's movement but rapidly became an activist with a new cause. Even a crusade. She went to look for books on genetics and Down's Syndrome at the Tawa Library. There weren't any. The librarian did not recognise the term Down's Syndrome but Lynne soon put her right.

When Duncan was four months old a 'dear little lady with a bun' arrived at her door and introduced herself as Jean Clark from the IHC. She had been given Lynne's name by a Plunket nurse. 'I came to see if you were all right.' Lynne joined the society there and then and Jean gave her a contact of a day-care centre attached to Campbell House adult training centre. She told Lynne: 'You are so lucky compared with parents in earlier years.'

Not feeling very lucky, Lynne took Duncan along to an IHC meeting, a morning tea group in the Porirua East Community Centre. 'There was a row of mums and six or seven Downies of various ages. We immediately started talking, made terrible jokes and in the end had a hilarious time.' For Lynne and Duncan it was the beginning of a new relationship; involvement with the IHC. Lynne soon became an organiser and in time an IHC branch official.

All IHC parents have a story to tell. Jamie was severely disabled and brain damaged as the result of an accident at the age of four. His mother Jeni remembers that during very low periods in her life there was always somebody associated with IHC ready to help.

> Years ago I was in the Wellington workshop dealing with multiply-handicapped people. The woman running the workshop was telling us how our children soon would all be using computers and I stood up and wailed at her, saying, 'How will you teach my son to use a computer when he can't swallow his own spit?' As I rushed out very upset I was approached by a very pleasant woman who asked if I would like to go home with her. I went to her home and sat by her daughter's bed and we cried and laughed. It was Gillian Deane.'

There was nothing new about the idea of parents helping one another, usually on an informal basis. It was in recognition of the importance of the value of this family-based support that IHC developed, in the 1980s, its concept of Shared Care. In part it was because the move against institutions was seeing families being encouraged to keep their disabled children at home, resulting in families coming under additional pressure, especially if additional resources were not available.

> We are expected, so the professionals tell us, to keep our children at home. They don't realise how this may affect our other children. We feel guilty for asking for help and support and for some reason we think that we should be the ones to take all the responsibility. We're not asking for someone to take over completely but it is nice to know that someone else will have an interest in your child and be there just to have a chat to every now and then.

A Shared Care pilot project undertaken in Wellington was described in the journal in 1985. It involved 'a family other than the family of the handicapped child providing short-stay care for the child. In the past this "relief care" has always been provided by IHC in its residential homes or at Puketiro Centre run by the Wellington Hospital Board.' Shared Care was becoming a reality in other regions. Representatives went to a public meeting in Gisborne in April 1986 to promote the idea. Caregiver Shirley Summerfield provided the following story:

> When I first cared for Aaron it was through Home Aid. I did not know Liz and Neil [Aaron's natural parents] very well at all. I feel this is relevant as it shows that we had to get to know each other, as well as getting to know Aaron, from the start. It is nearly a year now since we first met and in that time our family relationships, I'm sure, have been built on trust, honesty, reliability, awareness and good communication ... Liz and I have had to learn our limits, learn to trust and be honest, and to basically have confidence in each other ... When I've had Aaron for the day Liz and I will sit down over a cup of coffee and talk about the day's events. We are always excited when Aaron has achieved some feat and I do look forward to sharing with Liz any little thing Aaron has done.

Making Policy and Tea – Normalisation

> 'Community living is not an alternative to institutions; institutions are an alternative to community living.'   *Dr Gunnar Dywbad, 1983*

It was not until 1974 that the government imposed a moratorium on the expansion of psychiatric and psychopaedic hospitals. The severely handicapped were transferred from the psychiatric to psychopaedic hospitals, and many mildly and moderately handicapped people were discharged from both types of institution.

The drive for community rather than institutional living was part of the 'normalisation' debate. The society's policy was that people with intellectual disabilities should live as far as possible within the community, and it pressed for more government support in order to make this possible.

The term 'normalisation' was not in general use until the mid-1970s. The journal at that time explained:

> The principle of normalisation consists of a series of inter-related principles and programmes which seek to integrate the handicapped and devalued person into the mainstream of society, enabling his life to be as close as possible to that of persons of similar age and sex in his culture.

The 1978 conference had spent much time debating a working party draft agreement on a new statement of philosophy and policy, based on the United Nations Declaration of Rights and other internationally accepted documents. After further discussion and in the light of comments received in the next 12 months it went forward for adoption in 1979. As passed it committed the society to a policy whereby community services for the intellectually disabled would be available from 'the cradle to the grave'. Today, IHC's *Philosophy and Policy* is a core document underpinning all IHC's services and activities.

This period, the late 1970s and early 1980s, was one of incredible change for IHC. The rapid growth of services, the complexity of handling finances, properties and other assets was putting a great strain on branch committees and members who were all volunteers. More and more staff had to be employed to do the work that had previously been done by parent volunteers. The growing number of paid staff was part of a trend towards 'professionalism' and efficiency in both the care of residents in hostels and in administrative matters. Barbara Rocco, who in 1979 found herself on the committee of the Marlborough branch, remembers the transition period. She says it was understandable that members would feel dismayed and perplexed when after spending years giving their all to the branch, they found that people were being paid to do the work. 'Not only paid, but supplied with expenses and a car!' At the same time, because the early pioneering days had passed, older members felt that the branches were losing much of their old spirit of togetherness.

Barbara was a parent of a disabled child, Stefano, born in Venice where the Roccos were living in 1975. He was one of those babies who is hard to diagnose. At birth he had stopped breathing for a short period but that appeared not to have had any effect. It was only after the milestones were missed that the doctors

Barbara Rocco, national president IHC, 1994–.

Dr Roderick Deane, national president
IHC 1988–94. IHC LIBRARY COLLECTION

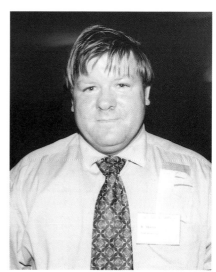

Robert Martin, national self-advocate.
IHC LIBRARY COLLECTION

David Corner, self-advocate adviser,
Southern Region. IHC LIBRARY COLLECTION

Angus Jones, office assistant, IHC national office, Wellington.

Moana Parker, office assistant, with JB Munro, national director/chief executive IHC 1977–97.

JB Munro, end of an era, 1997.

Jan Dowland, chief executive IHC (left), and Barbara Rocco, New Zealand president IHC, New Zealand Council,
Wellington 1999.

Lynne Renouf, president Mana branch, New Zealand Council, Wellington, 1999.   IHC LIBRARY COLLECTION

IHC patrons Roderick and Gillian Deane.   DAVID LEWIS

Searching a library database in the IHC Library, national office, Wellington.

IHC Library staff: library and information service manager Liz MacGibbon; librarian Annette Lane; library assistant Michael Holdsworth.

Mark Braam shows IHC chief executive Jan Dowland how he makes toy trucks at an IHC workshop in Dunedin, August 1999.

IHC Board of Governance 1999 (from top, left to right) Tony Shaw (NZ Vice President), Barbara Rocco (NZ President), John Holdsworth (NZ Vice President), Gary Child, Arun Amarsi, John Palmer, Jan Dowland, Roderick Deane, Dianne Bardsley, Donald Thompson, Susan Hughes, Bryce Quarrie.

IHC LIBRARY COLLECTION

IHC Executive Group 1999 (from top, left to right) Celia Dunlop, Ralph Jones, Jan Dowland (Chief Executive), Sharon Shipton, Jim Datson, Paula Comerford, Jeff Sanders, Janine Stewart, Carla Gini, Gordon Davies, Cliff Daly

IHC LIBRARY COLLECTION

began to figure out what was going wrong. Even when the family returned to New Zealand and settled in Blenheim it seemed possible that Stefano might 'catch up', but it was not to be. It was the visiting therapists at Wairau Hospital who were of most help to Barbara and Piero Rocco and they were in time able to make use of pre-school services for disabled children and a special unit attached to the primary school. At IHC Barbara most enjoyed meeting the older members and hearing them talk about the 'old days'.

Having started out as a rather reluctant committee member, within three years Barbara was attending New Zealand Committee meetings in Wellington as Marlborough regional representative. The meetings she recalls as exciting and scary. Government funding was inadequate for residential services. At the same time there had been an 11 per cent reduction in absolute numbers of people with an intellectual disability in institutions as families were encouraged to turn to other community-based options for their mildly and moderately handicapped members. More and more people were by then being catered for by IHC services, which were under continual pressure to keep up with the demands of families already shouldering a greater burden of care.

The growth of the Society's membership, the number of services and size of its operating budget (with capital assets by 1979 in excess of $10 million) had put large demands on the executive. At New Zealand Committee meetings in Wellington representatives found themselves coping with the need to balance the claims of various sectors: the need to provide residential services, to push the government on issues such as education and health, to manage the society's by now enormous assets and financial affairs and equally enormous debts. 'We were fearless in many ways,' Barbara recalled. 'There was a desperate, desperate need for more residential services in Auckland. We voted $1 million to buy 10 homes in Auckland. It was an act of faith – we didn't have the money, we just had to do it.'

In JB Munro the New Zealand Committee had a chief executive who endorsed their own view. He was an entrepreneur, adept at finding ways and means and believed that risks had to be taken. 'He would say yes, we'll do it and find the money somehow.'

De-institutionalisation

Changes in government policy owed as much to the government's desire to cut the costs of maintaining the institutions as to a new recognition that institutions were not the best place for many people. In 1986 it was estimated that 3000–4000 intellectually disabled people were living in psychiatric or psychopaedic hospitals. Increasing numbers were being discharged from the state institutions and despite the continual expansion of its operations, the society was hard pressed to cater for them and those who no longer entered such hospitals. The society continued to advocate community-based services and argued that the primary responsibility for providing them rested with the government. The first places built under the new government policies had tended to be large hostels, resembling the villas at Templeton and Kimberley. Later the policies changed and although the move was not without controversy, the society advocated smaller houses and began to replace the big hostels with smaller four- to six-bed homes scattered throughout the community.

Hospital boards began to buy up houses and move people into these homes. The Auckland Hospital Board announced a pilot for placing intellectually handicapped people in the community. In 1986 the journal reported that according to a Health Department spokesperson the concept of 'normalisation' was now widely accepted. It meant 'recognising the potential of the handicapped and giving them the opportunity to live in the same way as normal New Zealanders'. Many countries had already made the shift from institutions to community care: it was simply a matter of New Zealand catching up. The Director General of Health, Dr George Salmond, chaired a group including representatives of the Department of Health, hospital boards, IHC, parents' associations and the Public Service Association to discuss planning and policies to de-institutionalise psychopaedic and psychiatric hospitals. At its meetings in 1986 the group considered a seven-year plan for moving people out of the hospitals.

In September 1988 a Community Placement Action Group of three representatives each from the hospital board and IHC arranged for 54 Kingseat residents to be given the chance of community living. First came an assessment process and the completion of a 'Life Style Survey', and at the same time all parents or next of kin received a letter from the hospital informing them of the project. Decisions about the suitability of residents were made after discussion between the CPAG, IHC branch personnel, family members and the service users. Once the residents were moved into a new home an Individual Programme Plan meeting would review the suitability of the placement and identify goals to be worked on to ensure successful community integration.

Carolyn, aged 43 years, had lived at Kingseat for 28 years in a villa with over 30 people. Six weeks after moving into a five-bedroom house with staff support, she was assessed and considerable progress was noted. 'She is learning to make her lunch and is mastering the use of a knife and fork. She is becoming more independent with washing and dressing ... [and] ... has begun to walk to the local shop.' A major advantage for Carolyn was that she was now living closer to her 80-year-old mother, who could visit her for the first time in many years.

Frustration: Education Policy and Mainstreaming

'The Society remains angry and frustrated that it has been unable to persuade this government or the previous government to change the 1964 Education Act,' wrote Dr Terry Caseley in his president's report 1986. He added that the act 'discriminates against severely intellectually handicapped children in that it gives the Minister the power to exclude these children from the state education system. This is a blatant denial of a fundamental right – the right to education.'

The 1964 act had 'looked forward to adequate staff training schemes, to the development of opportunities for a career structure for teachers in this field of special education and to schools staffed by fully trained teachers'. None of these developments had taken place.

Although not without controversy by 1980 the society had adopted as official philosophy that children with an intellectual disability should be educated within the New Zealand schools system. Furthermore, 'each child's particular needs should be ascertained in full consultation with his or her parents and that the child be placed in an age-appropriate setting. For some children this may be in a regular classroom, for others it may be a special class or satellite class, while in some cases it may be a special school.' The society had the long-term goal of the demise of the special schools, with all children being integrated into regular schools.

So-called mainstreaming was not at that time government policy and it was considered a priority by the New Zealand Committee of the society to get the legislation changed. The society lobbied and received assurances from successive Ministers of Education and the Opposition spokespeople on Education that the act would be changed. We 'kept bellyaching about the need to get the Education Act changed,' recalled JB Munro.

It was one thing for the government of the day to make promises and commitments, but another for the words to become reality. By mid-1985 the promised amendment to the act had still not appeared and only five transfers of children with a disability into mainstream schools had taken place. Nevertheless, integration or 'normalisation' had started to happen in some areas. Otago's Macandrew Intermediate School had established a class for children with an intellectual disability in February 1985. The classroom proved inadequate but the Otago Education Board undertook to redesign the room, which, when finished had wheelchair-accessible toilet and washing facilities, handrails, ramps, non-slip flooring and adjustable-height tables. A teacher-pupil ratio allowed for one-to-one teaching in the integrated class, which provided opportunity of interaction among disabled and non-disabled school children and staff. The students in the disabled group had opportunity to work with specialist teachers and enjoyed woodworking, sewing and cooking as well as access to the facilities of the whole school: gym, hall, library, video room and canteen.

There were at that time approximately 300 school-age children in IHC facilities and an estimated 500–700 in the psychopaedic hospitals who were receiving little or no education. By 1988 there were 10 units in secondary schools, 22 units in intermediate schools and 58 in primary schools.

The long-awaited Education Act amendment finally was passed under the Labour government in 1989. People with a disability now had the same rights to enrol and receive education in state schools as people who did not. Gore branch president, Malcolm McDuff describes transitional problems faced at the time of mainstreaming when in accordance with IHC policy the branch closed its pre-school. 'We just about got killed. The pre-school was a secure situation that people didn't want to get rid of.' Pre-schoolers were in time integrated into local kindergartens.

Legacies and Landskills

A higher public profile and further injection of funds came with the 1981 International Year of Disabled Persons. JB Munro later recalled: 'The government wanted something organised for the IYDP ... [and] a general feeling amongst members of the co-ordinating councils and of voluntary agencies like CCS, IHC and the Foundation for the Blind was that there should be more co-operation and co-ordination.' It was agreed to try to establish a branch of Rehabilitation International and form an IYDP steering committee. The disability sector as a whole decided to make a bid for the proceeds of the 1981 Telethon – and succeeded. New Zealanders donated over $5 million, although applications for funds totalled $42 million. One of the outcomes was funding to enable the setting up of the Total Mobility Scheme and Teletext.

Fundraising at that period included a match-box scheme, Christmas card scheme, legacies, and the Sutherland Landskills Programme, made possible by the generosity of the Sutherland Self Help Trust Board, chaired by IHC patron John Sutherland. In 1985 Sutherland encouraged the society to apply to the trust board for a grant to help with some of its projects. In 1987 the annual report noted: 'Nobody within the organisation at that time [1985] could imagine the impact and the tremendous development which would result from a grant of $750,000 from the Sutherland Trust targeted specifically towards Agronomics.' The project devised was for the establishment of a national training school for intellectually handicapped adults in agriculture and horticulture. John Sutherland said that the project furthered the purpose for which the trust was set up: that of assisting those in the community less fortunate and less able to help themselves.

It was a blow to the society when their patron died in September 1986. But the idea of developing rural schemes that could involve disabled people in agricultural projects continued to flourish in many parts of New Zealand. The North Shore branch had opened a rural unit in 1981 on a 2.5-hectare property that had come to the society as the result of a legacy from John Richards. Nelson branch set up a similar rural training unit on a farm property bought at Richmond.

Gumboots for Calves

This unique fundraising scheme was the brainchild of Norman Cashmore from the Taranaki branch. He began the new initiative in 1982 in Taranaki, the heart of dairying country. In exchange for a pair of gumboots, farmers donated and reared a calf for the IHC. Through IHC networks Mick Murphy heard about

Norm Cashmore, the 'gumboot man'. He contacted Norm and after discussion they approached the New Zealand Committee with a plan for expanding the scheme throughout the country. The committee was hesitant at first, but in 1983 granted permission for Mick Murphy, who was based in Marlborough, to pilot a calf scheme in eight branches. Within two years the Society's annual report noted:. 'The calf scheme is proving to be a most successful innovation ... Although only a few branches participated, the trial run of the 1983–84 season resulted in 700 calves being sold.' Mick Murphy helped many other rural branches join the scheme, and used various methods to promote it. He endeavoured to find convenors in each branch and train them. Their role was to approach local farmers and convince them that the donation of a calf would benefit people with disabilities in their area. He stressed the importance of individual contact, 'to get the farmer to fill in the form there and then'. Former prime minister Bill Rowling, president of the Nelson branch, was one who promoted the scheme in that region. By 1985 Allflex International, the New Zealand Dairy Exporter, Skellerup Industries and Dalgety Crown all supported the IHC Calf Scheme. The response in the 1985–86 season was 'tremendous', with over 1700 calves donated to the society's branches raising more than $100,000.

Another boost to the plan came when Agrifeeds made their stand available to IHC at National Fieldays for farmers at Mystery Creek near Hamilton – the largest agricultural show in New Zealand. In 1987 Wrightson became official sponsor of the IHC Calf Scheme while the New Zealand Dairy Exporter continued its support by distributing pamphlets. The Golden Gumboot Award is won annually by the co-ordinator whose district has had greatest success in raising funds by this method and at the tenth anniversary celebration of the scheme six couples won trips to Australia. In the 1992–93 season the scheme for the first time reached the million-dollar target.

When Mick Murphy stepped down from his role as co-ordinator of this highly successful scheme he acknowledged the tremendous support he had received from Barry Baxter and Elly Knox of the IHC's Waikato West branch. In 1994 Barry Baxter, a Waikato farmer, took over as calf scheme co-ordinator, and he was followed three years later by Ian Gillard, Lakeland branch president. During his three years in the position donated calf numbers increased each year, to 5630 in 1997. The scheme's founder, Norman Cashmore, had by then retired to live in Mount Maunganui where he became a convenor for the mid-Bay of Plenty area. He died at age 91 in 1992.

6

The Long and Passionate Journey

Tough at the Top

In 1988 Dr Terry Caseley retired from the presidency after nine years in the position. The new president was Dr R.S. (Roderick) Deane, who had replaced Jack Brotherston as one of the two vice-presidents in 1983. His election to the vice-presidency at the Wanganui conference had been contentious. There were five nominations (four of them branch presidents) for the position. Auckland branch president Graeme Reid was an obvious choice: an eminent Auckland businessman who from 1978 to 1980 had also been president of the New Zealand Employers' Federation. He was at the same time honorary consul for Portugal and known for his encouragement of the wine industry, his interest in rose growing and as an author. For the second vice-president, Jack Brotherston began lobbying for Roderick Deane. The crunch came and, it is said, the word went around: 'If you want to control Munro, vote Deane.' Deane got the job. Roderick Deane had been encouraged to stand for office in the IHC by his wife Gillian, who was friendly with JB Munro. This was partly because of their daughters: Sharon Munro was one of the team of carers who looked after Kristen when the Deanes were away.

Roderick Deane joined the National Finance Sub-Committee in 1978 following his return to New Zealand from the International Monetary Fund. His vast business experience was invaluable and he and other experts involved in the society ultimately saved the organisation from financial disaster. As vice-president, Deane examined the financial situation of IHC and found severe problems aggravated by the growing operating costs of new facilities. Interest rates and staffing costs were escalating. A story is told of Caseley and Deane buttonholing Prime Minister Robert Muldoon at a function and delivering an ultimatum. 'If you can't give us more government subsidies, we won't be able to carry on. Here are the keys – you run it.'

In 1990 the society was led by Dr Roderick Deane as president, and vice-presidents Barbara Rocco and Sir Wallace Rowling. For 24 years, more than half of its existence, the society had been led by members of the medical profession. Now came a new look: the leadership consisting of parents who had first-hand experience of the needs of members, along with many other skills and attributes. Former Prime Minister Bill Rowling had been Nelson branch president and had a skilled eye for constitutional and financial matters. Barbara Rocco remembers how much she learned from him and others such as Graeme Reid, Angus Capic and Neil Taylor. She herself was a former teacher and restaurateur with a considerable record of community service in Blenheim. She became chair of the newly established Standards and Monitoring Services Committee involved in setting and monitoring standards for IHC residential services. When she rather diffidently accepted the position of vice-president she made her position quite clear: 'I will never be president.'

Torrid Times: 1990–92

'Last year in 1989-90, IHC incurred an overall excess of expenditure over income of $11 million which after allowing for depreciation represented a cash deficit of around $7 million.' With these words president Roderick Deane sent shockwaves through the membership at the 1990 AGM. Drastic measures were called for. Luckily they had the right man for the job.

After several years of unprecedented economic growth, in October 1987 the New Zealand sharemarket crashed. It was a prelude to a sustained period of economic hardship, when the term 'restructuring' took on a sinister meaning for many people who found themselves out of work. It was also the time when the IHC found that the years of risk-taking and living beyond its means with an overdraft that got bigger rather than smaller were over. It was the end of a dream run.

In 1989 the Labour government promised to adjust the subsidy rating for IHC salaries but the 1990 Budget failed to deliver. Deane and Munro went to see the Minister, Michael Cullen, who said: 'Don't worry, we'll get it in the Supplementary Estimates.' Nothing happened, except that the Labour government went out and National came in and wiped the Supplementary Estimates. By this time the IHC was $10 million overdrawn; desperate measures were needed. The new Minister of Social Welfare, Jenny Shipley (later Prime Minister) appointed an IHC Review Team headed by Venn Young, which reported early in 1991. It supported the IHC submission, which asked for the means to implement structures based on its philosophy 'which allows all New Zealanders irrespective of the nature of their intellectual handicap or other disability to be assisted to live ordinary lives in ordinary communities'.

Meanwhile, the overdraft remained. Eventually Roderick Deane, JB Munro and others worked out a scheme with the politicians and relevant government officials. It was said that Deane, who had years of experience in dealing with the finances of huge corporations such as ECNZ and Telecom spent more sleepless nights worrying about the IHC than about any of his other responsibilities. The government eventually made over $10 million to cover the overdraft in an interest-free loan, but with many provisos; the main one being that the loan had to be repaid at the rate of $1 million per year over 10 years.

In a special meeting of the New Zealand Council in 1989 Roderick Deane had laid the position on the line to the branch presidents. In the end they could only agree that 'downsizing' and drastic economies were necessary. The national office moved to the 15th floor of Willbank House, in downtown Willis Street, Wellington. In what the president referred to as a 'climate of change' the executive office structure was altered and several hundred paid employees lost their jobs. Later the Standards and Monitoring Services Board reviewed the restructuring process. Streamlining included such things as having one manager to take charge of several of the IHC residences instead of having one manager for each home. During the 1980s branches had been participating in a costly programme of property replacement. IHC philosophy and policy had continued to propound the view that in order to improve lifestyle opportunities, people should not live in large hostels where they had little privacy or space for themselves, but in small homes. Branches worked with the Housing Corporation to arrange the purchase of four- and five-bedroom houses and were at the same time disposing of large complexes. It was painful for older members who had worked so hard to obtain, equip and maintain the hostels to see them go, and this caused much heartache. During the years 1990 and 1991 the society sold and replaced the following residences: Raewyn Street, Northland (25 beds); Fraser Avenue, North Harbour (40 beds); Carrington Road, Central Auckland (20 beds); Kawaha Point Road, Rotorua (21 beds); Dorset and Glamorgan, Napier (20 beds); Glen Road, Stokes Valley, Lower Hutt (20 beds); Ratahua, Hartley Stanley, Marlborough (20 beds); Rongo-Tane, Christchurch (20 beds); 14 Sandringham Street, Oamaru, North Otago (10 beds); Corstorphine, Otago (38 beds); Mitre House, Gore (9 beds).

In July 1993 the Society announced structural changes.

> Acting on the request of the Minister of Social Welfare, the IHC NZ Council has agreed that from 1 July 1993 we split our service delivery management structure into a regional configuration to match the Regional Health Authority (RHA) system. Thus IHC services are now being delivered in the RHA regions, the regional offices being located in Auckland, Tauranga, Palmerston North and Christchurch.

Each region had a general manager who reported to the chief executive. Along with structural changes the following year, 1994, saw a name change from New Zealand Society for the Intellectually Handicapped (Inc.) to IHC New Zealand (Inc.).

As the large hospitals and psychiatric institutions closed one by one, IHC service providers had to work out how to meet the needs of people moving into the community. Porirua Hospital closed part of its residential facilities in 1996, affecting about 80 people with an intellectual disability. Peggy Jones, who had been a regional manager and quality adviser for IHC, came out of retirement to become an independent advocate for those affected. She said many parents were nervous about the closure and her job would involve 'listening to their concerns, showing them that there are good services available in the community and reassuring them that responsibilities will not be thrust back on the shoulders of parents'.

One parent recalled: 'On our first visit to the group home we went to the front door and instead of having somebody go to the office and sign in and then phone over, and somebody else opening the door, we just went up to the door and rang the doorbell ... opened the door and said: "May we come in?" and someone said, "The kettle is on."'

Real jobs!

As well as attending special or satellite classes in the primary and secondary schools, beginning in the 1980s, young IHC 'clients' attended polytechnic 'New Directions' courses and work experience programmes.

In 1988 Fay McDonald, a community placement officer with IHC Otago branch, contacted Terrieann Shepherd, owner-operator of the McDonald's Restaurant in Dunedin. Together they selected four people to commence training at the restaurant, but soon realised that they needed to develop a formal programme to train one person at a time. IHC staff would go to the workplace and gain hands-on experience of the McDonald's system and thus know how to support future trainees. In this way McJobs came into being: designed to meet both the employment rights of individuals and the requirements of a commercial enterprise. Jan Rutherford, formerly employed at an IHC workshop packing foodstuffs, was the first trainee. She received six months' training supported by IHC staff on a one-to-one basis. (This was later changed to a system in which support came from a fellow McDonald's employee with IHC back-up when required.) Jan began work three days a week, four hours a day, and soon was stationed in the lobby. She responded well to the challenge and was promoted to hostess. She loved her work.

After this success Terrieann Shepherd and Fay McDonald encouraged other restaurant outlets to join the McJobs training programme. As a result of the success of the pilot scheme in Dunedin, McDonald's restaurants and IHC developed a joint venture of supported employment for people with an intellectual disability in other centres. Fay McDonald was appointed by the society as New Zealand co-ordinator for McJobs and similar projects. Rosemary Raukura was one of those who received training for work in McDonald's Family Restaurant in South Auckland. She received the same training as other staff, but spread over a longer period of time: in her case one year. McDonald's supplied the job coach, the costs being split with the society. Three years later Rosemary, then aged 38, was chosen as 'Employee of the Month' for April 1995. 'She is a model worker and I wouldn't trade her for anybody,' said the manager.

In November 1988 Joan Dellow of Timaru, South Canterbury branch, left polytechnic and started work.

On 8 November I collected my case, smock, cooking apron and said goodbye to everybody. Then I went over to the IHC workshop shortly after 9 o'clock to Vicki Rolls. Vicki took me up to the hospital ... to the main kitchen office. I met Mrs McKenzie. She asked me have I had experience and I said "yes" ... I am working with friendly staff. The first week when I started I was cutting rhubarb and I cut my finger a little bit. Later I was cutting silver beet and I cut my thumb. The next day a knife fell off the trolley and on top of my foot. Mrs Anderson put a plaster on it and took me to outpatients. When I was waiting at outpatients I met two people I know and they asked me what was I doing there. I said, I am working in the main kitchens and they were pleased I was work-ing. I had two stitches and a local anaesthetic and went back to the kitchens later. In the afternoon I did eggs. Then I helped with the stores to put them away with Mrs Anderson. I caught the bus at ten past four to go into town.

Was Joan enjoying her job? 'Loving it.'

'Speaking up for Ourselves': Self-advocacy and People First

The climate of the 1980s saw the development of self-advocacy in a number of areas, including among people with an intellectual disability.

In 1983 Canterbury reported activities in promoting self-advocacy programmes within its own and other branches and also other institutions in the Christ-church area. The branch had then sponsored a regional self-advocacy conference held in July at Lincoln College. It was attended by 88 people from the South Island branches and Sunnyside and Templeton hospitals and the main points of discussion were politics, privacy and pay.

Two years later the annual conference reported on the achievements of the self-advocacy group, led by Colin McLeod. The group had gained representation on the working party drafting submissions on the Protection of Personal and Property Rights Bill. Members had also undertaken speaking engagements, were planning a New Zealand newsletter, and were discussing a basic pay scale for all disabled people.

Angus Jones remembers the humble beginnings of self-advocacy.

I recall when client committees were all the rage within the branches ... on Friday afternoons when the staff would hold their weekly chat sessions, the clients would be holding their own client meetings which were often held in the dining room. It was a chance for them to talk about what was on their minds and to raise issues that they felt needed addressing.'

Eventually a number of self-advocacy groups gradually linked up across the country and came under the general heading of People First, which spearheaded the advocacy movement within the society. The People First movement had been encountered by JB Munro in the United States in 1978 and Munro remembers that in 1984 he had to move fast to get People First New Zealand registered under the Companies Act. 'There was a political party wanting to call itself People First which we had to head off at the pass.'

In 1986 the Nelson branch organised and promoted paid work in the rural Nelson district for disabled people. At the time the manager of the Nelson branch, Shmuel Bar-Even said: 'The most normalising thing is pay.' By 1989 the society had a national People First/Self-Advocacy programme and most regions had their own People First groups operating locally. In 1993 New Zealand sent four representatives to the Third International People First conference in Toronto, Canada. One was Robert Martin, national co-ordinator for self-advocacy. Robert was born in Wellington in 1957. At an early age his parents found they could not manage him and he was sent to Kimberley. There he had no schooling, making his own fun, and much mischief. It was only in sport that he found enjoyment and had some success. He was fostered out several times, unsuccessfully, and also had a period back at home with his parents and siblings. It was when working at an IHC establishment in Wanganui that Robert, who had in his own words 'always been a bit of a stirrer', began to use this part of his nature in a more positive way to help others. One of his first successes was to address issues of health and safety for IHC work and arrange for day base workers to get afternoon tea. He and other self-advocates also campaigned to get more money for their work. A keen sportsman, Robert Martin once biked to Palmerston North to raise money for Telethon and was selected to compete at Special Olympics in the United States. In the last few years he has become spokesperson for self-advocates in New Zealand and overseas. Robert Martin has achieved international recognition. He was elected onto the Council of Inclusion International in 1996 and today serves as third vice-president.

In 1993 when the People First logo was launched, Roderick Deane accompanied the self-advocates on their march to Parliament – the only time Deane has ever marched in the streets of Wellington.

Inclusion International

New Zealand has supported many projects in Asia and maintained contacts in other parts of the world. When Dr Donald Beasley ended his term as president in 1978, G.D. Wills as a member of the New Zealand Committee became part of the New Zealand delegation to the ILSMH (International League of Societies for Persons with Mental Handicap) World Congress in Vienna in 1978 and in 1994 was elected chair of SPANZ, the South Pacific arm of the International League of Societies for Persons with Mental Handicap. ILSMH changed its name to Inclusion International and now represents some 200 organisations in 120 countries advocating on behalf of 50 million people with an intellectual disability. When Don Wills in 1994 became third vice-president of Inclusion International he succeeded Graeme Reid, who had served for 12 years. In 1998 Wills became president, the second New Zealander – after Dr Beasley – to have held this position. When Robert Martin became third vice-president, Don Wills commented: 'The self-advocates have shown that we parents have to take a look at ourselves and be more ready to give up some of the constraints we put on our sons and daughters.'

Women at the Helm

'Rod Deane called me into his office for a secret meeting.' In 1994 Barbara Rocco heard the unwelcome news. Deane was planning not to seek re-election and furthermore he thought she should be the next president of the IHC. Her initial reaction was to the point: 'Get off the grass.' Hardly a surprising reaction from someone who only a few years earlier had said: 'I will never be president.' It happened, however, that Graeme Reid who had been destined for the job had withdrawn on grounds of ill-health. Roderick Deane was now looking to Barbara and he was not a man to take no for an answer.

By now the 'torrid' years were over. Though money was still very tight, and government policies were making life in the health and education sectors even more complicated, the new president took over a well-run organisation, with management on an even keel. Even so, when Roderick Deane resigned after six years it was a steep learning curve for Barbara and she was grateful for the help of her two vice-presidents, Neil Taylor and John Holdsworth. And of course the indefatigable chief executive JB Munro.

But more changes were in the offing in the fast-moving world of the 1990s. Munro at 61 retired from his position as chief executive in 1998 after 20 years in the job. Who would fill his busy shoes?

Another woman. Jan Dowland had the qualifications for the job, both academic and professional, and had already spent four years with the IHC as general manager of IHC Central Region. Then in her early forties, Jan Dowland was a graduate of Victoria University of Wellington with a first-class honours degree in psychology and an accountancy qualification. Her professional experience included management and research in the Department of Health and she had considerable experience in the disability sector. She had met JB Munro in 1987 when she began work at Ernst & Young. As always JB was on the lookout for talent that might be put to good use for the IHC and eventually he persuaded her to join the movement. As she said when she took over: 'The threads of my life have now been neatly pulled together to fully prepare me to run a care-giving charity in a businesslike way.'

Businesslike she needs to be. As it approaches its 50th anniversary the IHC has an annual budget of $130 million, a staff of 5000 and responsibility for more than 4000 people with an intellectual disability and their families.

The challenge for the IHC, as Barbara Rocco and Jan Dowland are both keenly aware, is to balance the needs and expectations of families, to provide independence but also support and advocacy for the most vulnerable, and to provide an effective voice to the nation. 'We must always be willing to take a risk, to be fearless.'

The Long and Passionate Journey

In 50 years IHC has evolved through various names, and from volunteer secretaries, through part-time secretaries, to branch administrators, branch managers, area managers, service managers and advisers. The people for whom the members have worked to provide services and a life of quality, have been handicapped, disabled, challenged or impaired, and they have been clients, consumers, service users and self-advocates. Throughout the years the members, whether parents, guardians, supporters or carers, have remained members – the backbone of the organisation, volunteers, unsung heroes, doing the hard work at the local committee level. Without the members, and especially the parents, there would be no IHC movement in New Zealand. In the words of Dr Beasley: 'The driving force must always be parents. They are the passionate membership ... we could never have done what we've done if it had not been for parents.'

Since 1949 the IHC in New Zealand has come a long way. The amazing progress has only been possible through a tremendous amount of public support and goodwill. New Zealanders now accept that people with an intellectual disability have the right to live in, and to be part of, their local community along-side their fellow citizens, with the same rights and privileges. As IHC New Zealand president Barbara Rocco has said: 'Young parents today quickly hook into the idea that their child be included in regular community activities. For me to reach that viewpoint has been a long journey.' Because of all those members who have had the courage of their convictions and who have worked to make them a reality, the IHC movement will continue its journey into the new millennium with hearts full of hope, resolute and unafraid.

1

The Changing Language of Intellectual Disability

In the early days of New Zealand colonial society little distinction was made between intellectual disability and mental illness. (Some of this confusion persists today.) Early legislation reinforced the belief in similarity and until 1922 the only state provision of services for those children and adults suffering an intellectual disability was in the mental hospitals. In 1929 Templeton and then Levin (1945) were opened as 'mental deficiency institutions' to provide separate accommodation for 'lower grade mental defectives'.

At the time of the first meeting of the Intellectually Handicapped Children's Parents' Association (IHCPA) in 1949, the Mental Defectives Act 1911 was still the current legislation dealing with intellectual disability. The definitions of the various grades of mental defect contained within the act were based on equivalent British legislation:

Mentally Subnormal

Dullard: a person of less than average intelligence, who may yet be regarded as falling in the lowest part of the range of normal intelligence.

Mental Defective: a person with a condition of arrested or incomplete development of mind existing before the age of 18 years, whether arising from inherent causes or induced by disease or injury.

Mental defectives were further subdivided into:

FEEBLE-MINDED: Persons who may be capable of earning a living under favourable circumstances, but are incapable from mental deficiency existing from birth or an early age of competing on equal terms with their normal fellows or of managing themselves and their affairs with ordinary prudence.

IMBECILES: Persons who though capable of guarding themselves against common physical dangers are incapable, or if of school age will presumably when older be incapable, of earning their own living by reason of mental deficiency existing from birth or an early age.

Idiots: Persons so deficient in mind from birth or an early age that they are unable to guard themselves against common physical dangers and therefore require the oversight, care, or control required to be exercised in the care of young children.

Idiots and imbeciles were spoken of together as 'lower-grade mental defectives'.

When it came to schooling and education administration, mentally defective children were further classified into:

Special Class Children

Those who are capable of undertaking modified activities and studies at the level of the Primers and Standards 1–4, not, however, in an ordinary school, but in a special class, where they are taught by special and protracted methods and given a greater measure of individual attention than is usual in an ordinary school. Their intelligence quotients lie as a rule between 50 and 75.

This group corresponded to the medical terminology of feeble-minded.

Occupational Centre Children

Those who are incapable of undertaking the activities and studies of special classes, but nevertheless can be trained to some extent in social habits and simple tasks. Their intelligence quotients, as far as they can be measured, lie as a rule between 20 and 50.

This group corresponded to the 'imbeciles' of the medical and legal definition.

On the advice of the government psychologist of the time, the fledgling IHCPA adopted the term 'intellectually handicapped' instead of 'mental defective', current at that time. The early constitution defined intellectual handicap as covering 'any child whose mental or educational development is hindered or prevented by reason of physical or mental defect' and was extended to 'adult persons who have suffered from such defect in childhood and continue so to suffer'.

The term 'intellectually handicapped' met with opposition from government and other officials, who considered it to be an 'unsatisfactory term'. However, government officials did concede that it had one advantage in that it did not have the derogatory connotations of the words 'imbecile' or 'idiot'. A major disadvantage from their viewpoint was that the term included those people they labelled as idiots as well as imbeciles, 'so that it cannot be used as a gentler alternative to the latter'.

The term 'intellectual handicap' continued to be used until 1994 when it was changed to intellectual disability, partly to prevent continued confusion with mental illness. While 'intellectual handicap' has been widely used in New Zealand, elsewhere 'mental handicap', 'mental retardation' or 'learning disability' are more commonly used.

During the 1970s New Zealand adopted the World Health Organisation's five categories of mental retardation. These categories were based on tests of the individual's skills in language and academic situations only (intelligence tests) rather than a combination of academic and functional skills and involved individuals being classified as borderline, mild, moderate, severe or profoundly handicapped.

In recent years the language of disability has moved away from the medical approach to a social perspective that reflects the relationship between the individual and his or her environment. As our knowledge of intellectual disability increased, it became essential to include functional and adaptive skills alongside academic skills in assessments. This led to correspondingly improved language that placed more value on the individual and stressed positive values rather than the negative images conjured up by previous language use.

There has been much controversy over what is the best language to use. When the World Health Organisation updated its earlier categories of mental retardation in the 1980s and introduced definitions of key words, its definitions were considered controversial, even though they provided a useful guide to the differences between 'impairment', 'disability' and 'handicap' and have been used extensively around the world.

IHC's current *Philosophy and Policy* document defines intellectual disability as occurring when a person's intellectual functioning is well below average and he or she has difficulty learning daily life skills. These limitations – which can affect formal learning, communication, self care, social skills, health, work, and leisure – often exist alongside other abilities. With appropriate support, people can learn the skills necessary to participate in the community.

Intellectual disability is surrounded by negative myths and beliefs that reinforce prejudice and lower expectations. The terminology we use might not seem to matter on the surface, but to many people with disabilities and their families it is very important because it says much about the people or organisations that use it.

IHC has worked hard since its beginnings to change the attitudes of others towards people with intellectual disabilities and this is reflected in its drive to use language that values individuals and their place in the community.

Sue McKinnon
Advocate, IHC

References
Aitken, R.D. et al (1953): *Intellectually Handicapped Children*. Report of the Consultative Committee to the Minister of Education, Wellington.
Burns, C. et al (1959): *The Mental Deficiency Services: An Analysis of Existing Policy and the Community's Requirements.*
IHC New Zealand Incorporated (1996): *Philosophy and Policy.*
IHC New Zealand Incorporated, Centre for Learning (1996): *Introductory Training.*
Intellectually Handicapped Children's Parents' Association: *Constitution.*
Morrison, A. A., Beasley, D.M.G., Williamson, K.I. (1976): *The Intellectually Handicapped and their Families: A New Zealand Survey.*
Organisation of Services for the Mentally Retarded: Reports of the WHO Expert Committee on Mental Health (1968), (1984), Geneva.
Words Matter: A Guide to the Language of Disability. NZ Disabled, Auckland.

2

Milestones in IHC's History

- Winning the right to have family members at home – not in institutions

- Winning the right to have children included in regular schools

- Legislative changes to allow hostels

- Move from hostels to a wide range of integrated community living options:
    - Supported living
    - Contract board
    - Group homes
    - Flats attached to homes
    - Groups of flats

- Shift in acceptance from:
    People with intellectual disability can do little, to acceptance that every-one with an intellectual disability can be engaged in worthwhile work or activities.

- Emergence and growth of family support services:
    - Holiday programmes
    - Sibling camps
    - Parent advocacy groups
    - Home support
    - Respite care through shared care

- Training opportunities
    - Shared care
    - Advocacy
    - Education and educational issues
    - Behaviour support

Achievements for People with Intellectual Disabilities 1949–99

IHC advocacy at a national level and in local communities significantly influenced the following developments:

- The funding of services in the community for people with an intellectual disability was approved by the government in the early 1970s.
- De-institutionalisation of services for people with disabilities.
- The Disabled Persons Community Welfare Act, 1975.
- Mainstreaming in schools.
- Acceptance by government funders that smaller-scale houses were preferable to large hostel accommodation.
- Inclusion in the Human Rights Commission Act 1990 of people with an intellectual disability. (The first act excluded them specifically.)
- Education to enable the invalid benefit and disability allowance to be made available more readily to people with intellectual disabilities.
- The right for those with a permanent disability not to be required to undergo annual medical review for certain benefits.
- Protection of Personal and Property Rights Act, 1988.
- Availability of government housing for people with disabilities including modifications.
- Education Act 1989. Prior to this Act, a large number of children with intellectual disabilities were prevented from attending school.

4

Governance – Overview Since 1949

	1949–1950s	1960s and 70s	1980s and 90s	Today
Features	• Revolt against current thinking by families and a few enlightened professionals. • Access to educational opportunities.	• More powerful unified voice. • Start of service provision (with a lot of local involvement).	• More acceptance outside IHC of community living concept. • IHC as major service provider. • Growth of self-advocacy. • Growth of bureau-cracy (internal and external). • IHC as powerful lobbying force.	• Urgent need to strengthen local advocacy. • Need to reaffirm function of local and national committees. • IHC large business with revenue in excess of $130 million.
Governance	**IHCPA** *(Intellectually Handicapped Children's Parents' Association)* • Small parent groups banding together.	**NZSIH** *(New Zealand Society for the Intellectually Handicapped)* • 30+ branch committees. • 9–10 regions. • NZ Committee of Regional Reps. • Regional meetings for information sharing but not decision-making.	**IHC** • Approx. 50 branches. • New Zealand Council of Branch Presidents. • Some ad hoc regional groupings.	• Board of Governance established. • New Zealand Council of Branch Presidents meets less frequently. • Return to regional forums.
Management	• Almost nil – some secretarial positions.	• Branches – moved from having secretaries to paid administrators. • National director. • Some tension between committees and paid staff.	• Branches – areas. • Various regional groupings. • Decision making more formalised. • Taking over of many functions previously undertaken by branch committees.	• Areas – some service streaming. • Increasing professionalism. • Development of management culture. • Increasing funding constraints.

Formation of Branches

1950s
Wellington (1949), Auckland (1950, with four sub-branches), South Auckland (1950, with 12 sub-branches), Gisborne/Wairoa (1950), Wanganui (1950), Manawatu (1950), Southland (1950), Canterbury (1950), South Canterbury (1951), Otago (1951), North Taranaki (1951), Whangarei (1951), Franklin (1952), Wairarapa (1952), North Shore (1953), Nelson (1955), Tauranga (1957), South Taranaki (1959), Buller (early 1950s, but went in to recess mid-1950s)

1960s
King Country (1960), Marlborough (1960), Westland (1961), Rotorua (1961), North Otago (1962), Eastern Bay of Plenty (1962), Napier (1963), Hastings (1964), Ashburton (1965), Horowhenua (1968), Rangitikei (1969), Buller (1969)

1970s
Thames Valley (1971), Waikato (1975), Gore (1979)

1980s
South Auckland (1984), Eastern Auckland (1984), West Auckland (1984), Central Auckland (1984), Hutt Valley (1984), Manukau (1985), Tamaki (1985), Papakura/ Manurewa (1985), Waikato South (1985), Waikato West (1985), Hamilton East (1985), Tauranga East (1986, became Mid Bay of Plenty 1989), Christchurch North, South and West (1987), North Canterbury (1987), Upper Hutt (1987), Mana (1987), Clutha (1988), Lakeland (1988), Rangitoto (1988), North Harbour (1988), Cornwall (1988), Howick/ Pakuranga (1988), Far North (1988)

1990s
Kaipara (1992), South East Auckland (1995), Rodney (1995), Christchurch (1996), Kapiti (1997)

Decades of Change

	1950	1956	1969	1979	1989	1999
IHC Pre-school centres	1	2	15	50	44	None
Number of children	5	14	250	738	504	None
Occupational groups and special care centres		14	11	14		None
Number of people attending		100	109	152		None
Workshops and vocational centres			20	51	140	195
Adults attending workshops or vocational centres			480	1896	4437	4000
People in supported employment					300	433
Hostels and group homes	1	6	10	74	550	650
People living in IHC homes	1		220	761	2817	3200
Home support services (No. of hours)					14,322	170,527
Staff (full-time equivalent)			275	1000	2030	2900

continued

	1950	1956	1969	1979	1989	1999
Annual budget		£12,657	$616,958	$11m	$74.5m	$135m
National appeal			$279,034	$826,775	$977,342	$1.2m
Fundraising			$1046	$1.3m	$6.1m	$7.2m
Branches	April: 5 Dec.: 13	16	23	32	50	48
Membership	500					5000

Supported employment figures for 1989 include all people involved with supported employment even if only working for one morning a week.

7

Patrons, Presidents and Life Members 1949–99

Notes:

1. As appointments were made at AGMs held towards the end of each year, dates of appointment have been recorded for the first full year of their term of office – for example if appointed at the AGM in October of 1960, then the president is listed here as taking office from 1961. Period of office continued until the date given for the next appointee.

2. While time has gone into checking the accuracy of most dates listed, there have been instances when we have had to rely on people's memories.

3. In a number of instances branch records are incomplete. If you are able to fill in any gaps or make corrections, this information will be gratefully received by Liz MacGibbon at the IHC library at National Office, Wellington.

New Zealand Council

PATRONS: Sir William Perry (1960), Sir Clifford Plimmer (1969), John Sutherland (1983), Sir Paul Reeves (1987), Sir Wallace Rowling (1990), Dame Kiri Te Kanawa (1994), Dr Roderick and Mrs Gillian Deane (1998)

PRESIDENTS: Mr H.S. Anyon (1949), R.W.S. Botting (1954), Dr D.M.G. Beasley (1964), Dr R.T.M. Caseley (1980), Dr R.S. Deane (1990), Mrs B. Rocco (1995)

LIFE MEMBERS: H.S. Anyon, Mrs M. Anyon, Mrs L.I. Ranby (all awarded prior to 1960), J. Clark (1961), R.W.S. Botting and Mrs M. Botting (1966), Mr J. Nicholls (1972), Mrs O.M. Grenfell (1973), A.G. Crowe (1974), J.D. Burn-Murdoch (1980), K.I. Williamson (1981), G. Palmer (1981), Dr D.M.G. Beasley (1981), J.B. Brotherston (1983), R.G. Mathews (1983), Dr R.T.M. Caseley (1988), G.D. Wills (1994), Dr R.S. Deane (1996), J.P. Murphy (1996), N.A. Taylor (1998)

Northern Region

Northland Branch

PATRONS: Mrs J. Ryan (1985), Dr D.M.G. Beasley (1990)

PRESIDENTS: L. Blomfield (1951), Dr D.M.G. Beasley, (1971), A. House (1975), K. Gray (1988), Mrs W. McGlinchy (1990), Mrs A. Whitfield (1991), Mrs P. Day (1993)

LIFE MEMBERS: E. Cummings, Mrs Hallmond, Mrs P. Francis, A. House, Dr D.M.G. Beasley, L. Blomfield

Far North Branch

PRESIDENTS: C. West (1989), Mrs G. James (1991), R. Jameson (1993), B. Quarrie (1997)

LIFE MEMBERS: Mr W. and Mrs V. Simpson

Kaipara Branch

PRESIDENTS: R. Buckthought (1992–93), R.B. Sheridan (1994–95)

Auckland Branch

PATRONS: Mrs B. Goodman (1978), Mr C. Kay (1981) (last two patrons before the branch split)

PRESIDENTS: E.S. Woolley (1950), S. Luker (1952), E.L. Wood (1960), S. Luker (1964), M.L. Younger (1966), J.G.S. Reid (1976), G.D. Wills (1978–84)

LIFE MEMBERS: Mr and Mrs S. Luker, Mr and Mrs R.W. Tute, C.N. Nicholls, Mrs H. Ramsay, L.W. White, J. McKenzie, Mr and Mrs W. Grieve

1984 saw the Auckland branch split into four branches: South, Eastern, West and Central Auckland.

South/East Auckland (Manukau) Branch

1989 saw the Manukau branch split further into Manukau and Howick/Pakuranga, and then rejoined in 1995 to become South/East Auckland. The president was sometimes the same person for both branches.

Manukau

PRESIDENTS: J. Ansley (1985), Mrs G. Simmons (1994), B. Wilson (1997), Mrs S. Parks (1998)

PATRONS: Sir Barry Curtis (1995)

LIFE MEMBERS: Mrs S. Parks (1998)

Howick/Pakuranga

PRESIDENTS: R. Hider (1989), J. Hoyte (1992), J. Ansley (1993), Mrs G. Simmons (1994)

Eastern Auckland (Tamaki) Branch
PRESIDENTS: J. Borkin (1985), A. Best (1989)
LIFE MEMBERS: J. Fitzgerald, W. Hari

Cornwall Branch
PRESIDENTS: R. Martin (1989), D. Carter (1990), T. Kiely (1991), R. Leach (1992)
PATRON: Lady Fletcher (1988?–97)
LIFE MEMBER: J.G.S. Reid
Cornwall and Tamaki branch committees combined to become Cornwall/Tamaki in
    1996. Cornwall and Tamaki branch services are part of the South East Auckland
    branch.

West Auckland Branch
PRESIDENTS: A.E. Wood (1985), Mrs M. Wood (1986)
PATRON: J. Bateman

Central Auckland Branch
PRESIDENTS: R. Powell (1985), Mrs L. Hand (1989), J. Bateman (1991), A. Skiffington
    (1992), A. Gibbs (1992)
PATRON: Dame Cath Tizard (1991–93)
LIFE MEMBERS: W. Grieve, T. Piggin, J. Bateman, R. McKenzie
The Auckland Central branch combined with the West Auckland branch in 1993 to
    become West/Central Auckland, Mrs M. Wood as president.

Papakura/Manurewa Branch
PRESIDENTS: E.R. Snell (1985), J. Cobb (1988), C. Waigth (1991)
LIFE MEMBER: C. Waigth

North Shore Branch
PRESIDENTS: Mrs R. Woods (1953), J.C. Faithfull (1967), R.C. Stancich (1971),
    I.W. Rumsey (1974), O.A.S. Gale (1978), R.L. Davis (1981), D.C. Templeton (1984)
PATRON: N.J. King (1960–1988)
LIFE MEMBER: Mrs R. Woods (1971)
In 1988 the North Shore Branch split into the North Harbour branch and Rangitoto
    branch.

North Harbour Branch
PRESIDENTS: Mrs R. Gale (1988), Mrs M. Curle (1989), Mrs C. Rovers (1993),
    Mrs I. Sadler (1995), J. Palmer (1996)

PATRON: N.J. King (1988)

LIFE MEMBERS: O.I. Jones, R. Stancich, Mrs R. Gale (all awarded in 1988), N.J. King (1997)

Rangitoto Branch

PRESIDENTS: D. Templeton (1988), D. Hawke (1991), Mrs D. Herring (1995), K. Kennedy (1999)

PATRONS: M. McCully (1997)

LIFE MEMBERS: J.C. Faithfull (1988), D. Templeton (1991), B. Collett (1992)

Rodney Branch

PRESIDENTS: Mrs E. McNickle (1995), K. Conning (1996), Mrs V. Shepherd (1998)

Franklin Branch

PRESIDENTS: H.W. Barnaby (1952), A.L. Brownhill (1957), D. Hodder (1963), N.H. Kidd (1965), K.S. Jones (1976), M. Evans (1978), G. Harris (1979), M. Irwin (1986), P. McCormick (1987), M. Irwin (1990), M. Moloney (1992), R. Liddell (1993), M. Moloney (1997)

PATRONS: M. Wellington, Sir William Birch

LIFE MEMBERS: Mr and Mrs Brownhill, J. Johnson, E. Atger, G. Barnaby, M. Evans, K. Jones, Mrs J. Kidd, N.H. Kidd, Mrs E. Shoesmith

Midland Region

North Taranaki Branch

PRESIDENTS: L. Ivel (1951), J. Nicholls (1955), M. May (1957), L. Ivel (1958), M. May (1960), A. Watt (1965), J. Nicholls (1969), A. Watt (1970), D. King (1974), G. Cooke (1981), E. Riddick (1988), I. Russell (1991)

PATRONS: J.A. Nicholls (1970–78), A. Watt (1979–82), D.V. Sutherland (1984–92)

LIFE MEMBERS: Mr Alderson (1954), J. Nicholls (1970), M. Kay, Mrs R. Kay (1970), Miss K. Todd (1973), Lady Matthews, Mrs B. Jury, S. Hayton, J. Chivers, Mrs P. Allen (1981), Miss L. Taylor (1983), D. King (1990)

South Taranaki Branch

PRESIDENTS: J.A. Atkins (1959), N.M. Hislop (1960), H. Dormer (1962), J.A. Graham (1963), J. Morrison (1968), Mrs E. Crosby (1969), M. Boyd (1978), A.P. Ramsay (1982), N.A. Taylor (1986), Mrs D. Bardsley (1996)

PATRONS: Mr and Mrs Murray (1979), Mr C. Smith (1986)

LIFE MEMBERS: Mrs E. Crosby, C. Greaves, Mrs D. Hagen

King Country Branch

From 1960 to 1976 King country was a sub-branch of the South Auckland branch.

PRESIDENTS: T. Aldridge, (1960), B.R. Woodall (1961), J.H. Hewitson (1965),
    J. Thomson (1966), G. Clark (1968), M. Button (1970), C.E. Meads (1973), P. Bailes
    (1976), C.E. Meads (1979), R. Bree (1986), Mrs M. Ingham (1987)

PATRONS: D.C. Seath (1960), J. Bolger (1971), C.E. Meads (1987)

LIFE MEMBERS: Mrs J. Boniface (1990), B. Howell (1994), Mrs P. Howell (1995)

Waikato West Branch

PRESIDENTS: B. West (1988), P. Grey (1998)

PATRON: Mrs B. Osmond (1988–99)

LIFE MEMBER: B. West

Hamilton Branch

Originally South Auckland branch (south of the Bombay Hills to Taupo) until 1975
    when the branch became firstly Waikato and then Hamilton (1990).

PRESIDENTS: J.D. Burn-Murdoch (1950), Mrs L.I. Ranby (1951), J.R. Murray (1954),
    J.D. Burn-Murdoch (1957), J.R. Murray (1958), Mrs L.I. Ranby (1960),
    J.C. Faithfull (1962), J.W. Brown (1962), L.H. Maber (1963) A.V. Griffiths (1966),
    H.A. Parsons (1968), T. Hickmott (1971), D. Tate (1975), G.D. Meyer (1977),
    Mrs V.D. Brown (1990)

PATRONS: D.V. Bryant (1954), J.C. Pollock (1962), Sir Douglas Carter (1965),
    W. Dillon (1983), Dr I. Shearer (1984), J.F. Luxton (1986), W. Dillon (1989),
    Miss A. McClay (1990), G. Thomas (1992)

LIFE MEMBERS: Mrs L.I. Ranby (1954), J.R. Murray (1967), T. Hickmott (1974),
    D.M. Tate (1978), R. Swarbrick (1981), Mrs I. Skelton (1981), P.S. Hanan

Waikato South Branch

PRESIDENTS: P.S. Hanan (1987), Mrs P. Corrigan (1991), D. Hogan (1992),
    Mrs M. Lamb (1998)

PATRONS: J.F. Luxton (1988), P.S. Hanan (1996)

LIFE MEMBERS: Mrs P. Corrigan, Mrs A. Davidson, Mrs P. Hanan, Mrs C. Nickel,
    Mrs H. Putt, Mrs S. Lalich, D. Hogan, D. McLean, K. Rea

Thames Valley Branch

PRESIDENTS: G. Watton (1971), Mrs G. Williams (1978), G. Watton (1979), M. Clarke
    (1985), Mrs B. Davis (1989), J. Boyd (1992), Mrs H. Joines (1997)

PATRONS: W. Hopping (1976), Mrs D. Ingley (1991), W. French (1997)

LIFE MEMBERS: Mrs G. Williams, Mrs D. Ingley, G. Watton, W. French

Mid Bay of Plenty

PRESIDENTS: Mrs J. Moran (1989), Mrs S. Payne (1997)
PATRONS: W. Moultrie (1989), N. Cashmore (1990), Mrs D. Gemming (1995)
LIFE MEMBERS: Mrs R. Andrews (1989), Mrs B. Freeman (1989)

Tauranga Branch

PRESIDENTS: D. Mitchell (1957), A. Murrell (1959), D.S. Nicholson (1965),
    D. Mountford (1966), D.S. Nicholson (1969), J.D. Burn-Murdoch (1970),
    L.H. Maber (1977), R. Hill (1979), R. Somerfield (1983), D. Johnston (1988),
    R. Somerfield (1991), Mrs A. Pritchard (1998)
PATRONS: Mrs T. D. Mitchell (1959), Mr and Mrs D. Mitchell (1964), Mrs T. Mitchell
    (1965), J.D. Burn-Murdoch (1977), Mrs K.D. Kirkby (1986), Rev. F. Hume (1991)
LIFE MEMBERS: Mrs Hitchcock (1966), J.D. Burn-Murdoch (1975), T. Lester (1979),
    Mrs M. Rimmer (1982), Mrs R. Andrews (1984), N. Freeman (1984), R. Hill (1988),
    Mrs B. Freeman (1989), Mrs T. Mitchell (1989), P. Morine (1993), G. Watts (1997),
    Mrs A. Watts (1997)

Eastern Bay of Plenty Branch

PRESIDENTS: D.S. Turnbull (1962), D.R. McAllum (1963), Mrs P. Cunninghame (1976),
    N.J. Richardson (1995)
PATRONS: H.J. Warren (1962), R.T. Morpeth (1981–85), J. Gow (1988-94)
LIFE MEMBERS: D.R. McAllum (1990), Mrs P. Cunninghame (1995)

Rotorua Branch

PRESIDENTS: Mrs O. Atkinson (1961), J. Pritchard (1969), J.W. Williams (1972),
    Dr M.R. Miles (1974), W. Coleman (1976), N.P. Farmer (1977), G. Spurdle (1980),
    Mrs M. Stewart (1983), M. Ryan (1986), R. Pedley (1990), Mrs B. Blezard (1994)
PATRON: G. Beale (1974)
LIFE MEMBERS: Mrs L. Quinn, G. Beale

Lakeland Branch

PRESIDENTS: I. Gillard (1988), K. Quinn (1998)
PATRONS: C. Bewley (1988), Mrs J. Williamson (1989)
LIFE MEMBERS: Mrs N. Erskine, I. Gillard

Gisborne/Wairoa Branch

All early records for the period 1949–1952 were destroyed in a fire.
PRESIDENTS: W.E. Donnelly (1953), A. Williams (1954), I. Smith (1955),
    Mrs E. Hickman (1961), I. Smith (1963), Mrs N. Steed (1967), N. Davies (1977),
    Mrs L. Porter (1979), Mrs D. Nisbett (1980), Mrs N. Steed (1987), Mrs P. Donnelly

(1989), R. Porter (1992), A. Mackintosh (1996)

PATRONS: H.B. Williams (1988)

LIFE MEMBERS: J. O'Donoghue (1976), Mrs N. Steed (1978), P. Pilbrow (1989),
J. McFarlane (1989), Mrs M. Sutton (1992), Mrs M. Dutch (1995), R. Porter (1998)

Central Region

Napier Branch

PRESIDENTS: R.A. Hilton (1964), B.S. Brinsley (1971), B. Hart (1983), Dr I. Hunter
(1984), R. Beck (1985), B. Hart (1986), B. Barbour (1987), Mrs B. Wilson (1990),
Mrs C. Charman (1991), P. Thompson (1993), F. Powell (1997)

PATRONS: D. Cockburn, G. Braybrooke, D. Marshall

LIFE MEMBERS: B.S. Brinsley, Miss Collett, R. Beck, Mrs M. Beck, J. Nixon,
Mrs I. Nixon

Hastings Branch

PRESIDENTS: A. Ross (1964), C.P. Fowler (1974), P.T. Lowe (1978), J.W. Hildred
(1981), H. Barr (1983), P. Dunkerley (1987), H. Donald (1988), J. Walker (1992),
Mrs M. Gaby (1997)

PATRONS: J.J. O'Connor, J. Dwyer, N. Wilson

LIFE MEMBERS: H. Barr, Mrs Barr, Mrs A. Fowler, A.G. Hutchinson, Mrs Hutchinson,
D. Love, Mrs Love, D.C. Miller, Mrs Miller, A. Ross, Mrs Ross, Mrs Boag

Wanganui Branch

PRESIDENTS: Mr Wilkie (1950), Mrs G. Rowe (1952), Mr McCashin (1954),
Mrs Uttley (1955), Mr Nicholls (1959), Mr Ashton (1963), V.R. Jones (1968),
J.B. Brotherston (1970), H.E. Wynne (1978), B.A. Schofield (1985),
Mrs B. Montgomerie (1987), Mr B. Stone (1991), M. Ward (1993)

PATRONS: Mr Andrews (1965), Mr Russell (1974), C. Poynter (1994)

LIFE MEMBERS: J.B. Brotherston, P. Ashton, Mrs J. Ashton, Mrs B. Montgomerie,
Mrs B. Bourke, Dr B. Stone, H.E. Wynne, T. Armstrong, P. Young, Mrs J. Young

Rangitikei Branch

PRESIDENTS: K.P. Oliver (1969), A.M. Fyfe (1970), O.D. Hughes (1971), Mrs M. Ellen
(1977), A. Willis (1979), M. Watson (1981–82), Mrs J. Johnston (1990),
R. Balcombe (1997), Mrs M. Hollingsworth (1998), T. Hanson (1999)

PATRONS: Mrs C. Clausen, Mrs S. Moody

Manawatu Branch

PRESIDENTS: Rev. V. Mead (1950), A.C. Philpott (1953), L.C. Bennett (1954), C.N. Houghton (1957), A. Forrest (1963), K.I. Williamson (1965), G.N. Stayt (1972), I. Richardson (1978), J. Bos (1979), K.I. Williamson (1981), Mrs H. Allan (1986), G. Child (1992)

LIFE MEMBERS: Mr Grant (1977), G.N. Stayt (1981), K.I. Williamson (1986)

Horowhenua Branch

PRESIDENTS: P.S. McKenzie (1968), R. Hubbard (1970), J. Lines (1978), M. Hayward (1981), L. Cooney (1986), L. Patterson (1988), R. Waterson (1989), P. Sullivan (1997), M. Bull (1998)

PATRON: Mrs J. Keall (1999)

LIFE MEMBERS: L. Cooney, Mrs M. Faith, R. Waterson, D. Spence, Mr and Mrs P.J. Barrett, Mrs C.M. Davidson, Mr and Mrs P.S. McKenzie

Wellington Branch

The Wellington branch committee acted as the New Zealand Committee between 1949 and March 1951. The Greater Wellington branch became Wellington/ West Coast and Hutt Valley in 1984 and further split in 1987 to become Wellington, Kapi Mana, Hutt Valley and Upper Hutt branches. Kapi Mana branch was renamed Mana branch in 1994, with Kapiti becoming a separate branch in 1997.

PRESIDENTS: H.S. Anyon (1949), G.L. Whyte (1955), E.D. Hodder (1957), R.T. Ordish (1958), Mrs J. Clark (1962), D. Best (1973), J. Kellow (1975), Prof. T.D.C. Cullwick (1978), R. Craig (1979), E.C. Templeton (1980), Mrs J. Heyes (1983), J.T. Judge (1985), A. Griffiths (1986), J. Laurenson (1988), J. Holdsworth (1994), Mrs R. Heather (1999)

PATRONS: C.H.R. Jepsen, Sir Clifford Plimmer (1969), J.B. Burke, Mrs D. Mills, I. Trask (all 1986-87), J. Belich (1988-1991)

LIFE MEMBERS: Mrs J. Heyes

Hutt Valley Branch

PRESIDENTS: H. Abel (1984), J. Forman (1998)

Patrons: R. Kirton, Sir John Kennedy-Good, Mrs E. Jakobson, R. Marston (1984-86), Sir David Beattie (1986), Mrs B. Evans (1988), Mrs K. Terris (1995)

LIFE MEMBERS: H. Abel (1990), Mrs N. J. Abel (1990), G. Glenday (1993), A. Winchester (1996), Mrs J. Winchester (1996)

Upper Hutt Branch

PRESIDENTS: M. Heyrick (1987), F. Vandervoorst (1991)

PATRON: R. Kirton

LIFE MEMBERS: C. O'Riley, Mrs J. O'Riley (1998)

Mana Branch
PRESIDENTS: A. Griffiths (1987), R. Belton (1991), S. Bright (1992), Mrs L. Outtrim (1993), Mrs L. Renouf (1994)

Kapiti Branch
PRESIDENT: A. Hawkins (1997)
PATRON: R. Sowry

Wairarapa Branch
PRESIDENTS: H. Ward (1952), A.A. Ward (1952), K.W. Wright (1960), H. McKenzie (1961), B. Martin (1962), M. Street (1963), L. George (1964), B. Davey (1970), Mrs J. Ussher (1973), G. Bews (1976), Mrs N. Oakly (1979), J. Jolliffe (1981), L. Henderson (1982), J.M. Jolliffe (1985), D. Esau (1986), Mrs M. Bradshaw (1990), C. Redvers (1995)
PATRONS: W.H. Booth (1952), H.V. Donald (1966)
LIFE MEMBERS: W. Gillies (1967), L. George (1972), Mrs N. Oakly (1977)

Marlborough Branch
PRESIDENTS: Mrs R. Heagney (1960), Mrs P. Ballinger (1967), R.C. Jones (1973), J.P. Murphy (1974), B. Rocco (1983), R. Gill (1990), A. Kingston (1992), G. Leov (1999)
PATRONS: Mrs P. Ballinger (1975), I. Colombus (1990)
LIFE MEMBERS: J.P. Murphy, I. Colombus, Mrs P. Ballinger, Mrs J. Shewan, Mrs R. Quinn, Mrs R. Heagney

Nelson Branch
PRESIDENTS: H. Rodgers (1955), H. Sharland (1959), H. Rodgers (1960), F.A. McIlroy (1968), P.A. Dodd (1972), W.K. Bryce (1977), R.W. Luff (1979), Mrs G. Sadler (1982), R. Morrison (1982), Sir Wallace Rowling (1984), Mrs B. Fish (1985), Mrs D. Willems (1987), G.A. Harris (1996)
PATRONS: Sir Wallace Rowling (1988), Sir Patrick Goodman (1996)
LIFE MEMBERS: H. Rodgers (1983), Mrs G. Solly (1983), Mrs D. Barclay (1989), C. Buckley (1989), M. Fairweather (1995), Mrs B. Fairweather (1995), Mrs B. Fish, Mrs G. Sadler, Mrs D. Willems (1999)

Southern Region
Southland Branch
PRESIDENTS: W.T. Granger (1950), J.P. Thompson (1952), K.M. Fraser (1954), J.P. Thompson (1956), S. King (1960), T. Henshall (1967), W.P. Devine (1973),

D.E. Little (1978), R. Miller (1983), K. Ward (1988), Mrs N. Lewis (1998)
LIFE MEMBERS: H.S. Anyon, Mrs M. Anyon (1954), Mrs I. Winwood (1964),
J. Robinson (1969), T. Henshall (1972), Mrs M. Neilson (1983), J.P. Thompson
(1990), W. Blain (1993), Mrs M. Blain (1993)

Gore Branch
PRESIDENTS: J. Speden (1979), D. Turner (1984), M. McDuff (1985), P. Goodger
(1997)
LIFE MEMBERS: J. Speden, D. Turner, T. Brydone, M. McDuff, Mrs D. Thayer

Clutha Branch
PRESIDENTS: W. Aldcroft (1988), G. Neale (1992), T. Goudie (1999)
PATRONS: Sir Robin Gray, K. Fyall
LIFE MEMBERS: W. Aldcroft, G. Neale

Otago Branch
PRESIDENTS: R.W.S. Botting (1951), B.V. Wright (1965), W.F. McCay (1971),
J. Walker (1975), I.A. Hope (1979), Mrs L. Stewart (1991), B. McCombe (1994),
Mrs M. Withnall (1997)
PATRONS: Sir James and Lady Barnes, E. Edgar
LIFE MEMBERS: Mrs A.A. Orton, W.R. Caird, Mrs I. Laidlaw, J. McKechie, Mrs A. Burt,
R.W.S. Botting, J. Walker

North Otago Branch
PRESIDENTS: E.G. Carter (1962), W.R. Patterson (1965), A. Rudduck (1967),
J.A. Kingan (1970), W.R. Patterson (1971), C.E. McLeod (1974), C.R. Dorsey (1987),
D. Thompson (1989)
PATRONS: A.D. Dick (1965), W.R. Laney (1972), R.D. Allen (1974), R.J. Denny (1978),
Mrs J.F. Chisholm (1987), D.R. Sim (1987)
LIFE MEMBERS: Miss D. Carson, C.R. Dorsey, W.R. Patterson, Mrs H.B. Gardiner

South Canterbury Branch
PRESIDENTS: H. Dennison (1951), T. Hartstein (1956), A. Crowe (1960), J. Cleland
(1966), O. Tubb (1969), D. Sampson (1971), N. Hitchens (1973), G. Palmer (1975),
I. Taylor (1984), Mrs L. Miller (1992), T. Shaw (1993)
PATRON: W. Raymond
LIFE MEMBERS: G. Nicholl, H. Dennison, A. Crowe, L. Farthing, Mrs S. Dennison,
G. Palmer, Mrs M. Newman

Ashburton Branch

PRESIDENTS: H.G. Douglas (1965), Dr B.J. Francis (1968) G. Palmer (1972), J. Babbington (1973), G. Campbell (1977), Mrs B. Wills (1981), T.A. Hart (1983), J. Falloon (1987), B.J. Keen (1992)

PATRONS: A.J. Mason (1968-71), H.G. Douglas (1981), Mrs M. Boucher (1985)

LIFE MEMBERS: Dr B.J. Francis, Miss E. Bradley, Mrs M. Boucher, Mrs B. Wills

Christchurch Branch

Originally Canterbury branch until 1987 when it split into Christchurch North, South and West branches and North Canterbury branch. In 1996 the three Christchurch branches combined again to form Christchurch branch.

PRESIDENTS: P. Griffiths (1996), J. Roland (1998), Mrs L. Steele (1999)

CANTERBURY: J. Keenan, F.V. Hallam, W. Clark, S.A. Roberts (1950s), C. Curragh, Dr R.M.T. Caseley (1960s), Dr R.M.T. Caseley, (1970), M.A. Lefebvre (1971), M. Burbery (1973), Dr R.M.T. Caseley (1977), G. Jones (1979), Mrs P.J. Hunter (1982), D.B. Moore (1985),

PATRONS: Mrs M.E. James, Ruth Richardson, Mrs M. Murray, J. Anderton, N. Graham, J. Hopkins (current)

LIFE MEMBERS: Mrs M. Soppet, Mrs T. Webb, Mrs B. Allardyce, R. Allardyce, Mrs M. Gray, Mrs M. Barrett

Christchurch West: Dr O. Webb (1987), P. Griffiths (1993)

Christchurch North: M. Southern (1987), J. de Leijer (1992), R. Dodge (1995)

Christchurch South: R. Wiggins (1987), Mrs J. Jennings (1992)

North Canterbury Branch

PRESIDENTS: D.B. Moore (1987), B. Chapman (1989), Mrs L. Sloss (1993), D. Sloss (1996)

PATRONS: J. Gerard, Janice Skurr (current)

Buller Branch

The Buller branch was first formed in the early 1950s but went into recess in the mid-1950s.

PRESIDENTS: N. Wright (1969), G. Berendt (1972), Miss J. McGreevy (1975), K. Powell (1977), Mrs P. Mullan (1982), Mrs A. Kilkolly (1986), J. Wilson (1989), Mrs V. Smalley (1997), Mrs C. Hartigan (1999)

PATRONS: R. Pratt (1969), K. Pratt (1989), Mrs J. Dellaca (1990), W. Mullan (1993)

LIFE MEMBERS: Mrs J. McGreevy, Mrs J. Halkett, K. Powell, Mrs P. Mullan, C. Hartigan

Westland Branch

PRESIDENTS: R. Bell (1961), C.R. Rollinson (1965), J.P. Thomson (1967),
   Miss J. McGreevy (1975), Mrs L. Strange (1976), F. Neame (1982), Mrs G. Campbell
   (1988), K. Edwards (1996)

PATRONS: Dr B.M. Dallas (1963), W.J. Clancy (1971), Mr and Mrs W.S. McClymont
   (1983), Mrs E. McClymont (1985), A.C. Ellery (1988)

LIFE MEMBERS: W. Frost (1982), C. Jefferies (1982), Mrs M. Leach (1985),
   Mrs D. Davidson, Mrs L. Ilton, Mrs G. Campbell

Timeline

1877	NZ Education Act
1907	Otekaike School for boys (later called Campbell Park School) opened, 40 miles west of Oamaru
1908	Lunatics Act
1911	Mental Defectives Act
1914	Mental Defectives Amendment Act; Education Act
1916	Salisbury School (Richmond) for girls opened
1917	Special class opened at Auckland Normal School
1921–22	Mental Defectives Amendment Act
1922	Committee of Enquiry into Mental Defectives & Sexual Offenders (Board of Health); Stoke Farm established
1924	Report (Pomare); eugenics debate
1928	Mental Defectives Amendment Act
1929	Templeton Farm and Training School opened
1935	Labour government elected; Keith Anyon born with Down Syndrome
1938	Social Security Act
1942	Anyons approach After-Care Association, Wellington
1944	Department of Health takes over air force base at Levin to establish Levin Farm
1946	Margaret Anyon becomes honorary secretary of After-Care Association. Association of Parents of Backward Children formed in Britain
1947	Margaret Anyon visits Dunedin to observe centre, resigns from After-Care Association, Wellington
1948	T.H. McCombs (Minister of Education) writes to Anyons re Education Board proposal to establish an occupational centre
1949	Formation of Intellectually Handicapped Children's Parents' Association (IHCPA). Meeting of 22 people on 25 October elects Interim Committee: H.S. Anyon (president); Margaret Anyon (secretary/treasurer); Mrs Olive Grenfell and Mr C. Outhwaite (committee)

	Second meeting 23 November at NZEI rooms in Willis St: 50 present. IHCPA (Inc.) formed: H.S. Anyon (president); Mrs H.L. Grenfell (vice-president); Mrs M. Anyon (secretary); T. Brydone (honorary treasurer); Mrs R. Morris, A.C. Buckley, R. Graves, C. Outhwaite (committee)
1950	Hilda Ross (Minister of Social Welfare and Women and Children) supports plan for school; IHCPA Dominion Conference 27 April
	Petition to Parliament (3294 signatures) presented 2 August 1950
1951	Second conference 1–2 March; committee set up to report to Parliament (Dr R.S. Aitken)
1952	Third annual conference 17–18 April; Correspondence School Home Training Section established
1953	*Intellectually Handicapped Children*: Report of the Consultative Committee (Aitken Report)
1954	WHO Technical Report No. 75; Kristina Home (Jepsen) opened; R.W.S. Botting elected president IHCPA; Mental Health Amendment Act; Annual conference, Auckland
1955	Anyons resign from IHCPA, 2 May
1958	BMA NZ Branch: Mental Deficiency Sub-Committee
1959	BMA NZ Branch Report (Sir Charles Burns)
1960	Disabled Persons Employment Promotion Act. Dr D.M.G. Beasley undertakes overseas study sponsored by government
1961	Annual conference, Whangarei
1962	Name change to Intellectually Handicapped Children's Society (IHCS)
1964	Education Act; Dr D.M.G. Beasley elected president; annual conference, Nelson
1965	IHCS publishes *Community Care of the Intellectually Handicapped*. H.S. Anyon dies; annual conference, Hastings
1967	Annual conference hosted by North Shore branch
1968	Full-time branch administrators appointed: Maureen Tilly (South Auckland); Don Hodder (North Shore), JB Munro (Southland); Wairarapa branch hosts annual conference, Masterton
1969	Auckland branch administrator appointed; South Auckland branch hosts annual conference, Hamilton
1970	IHC 21st anniversary; Royal Commission on Social Security; Marlborough branch hosts annual conference, Blenheim
1971	UN Declaration of Rights; M.S. (Lofty) Blomfield dies; annual conference, Palmerston North
1973	Asian Federation for the Mentally Retarded first meeting in Manila, attended by NZ Committee representatives; annual conference, Tauranga
1974	Dr Beasley elected president of International League of Societies for Persons

with Mental Handicap; IHC 25th anniversary; South Pacific conference of the International League of Societies for the Mentally Retarded, Wellington, 25 October

1975   Name change to New Zealand Society for the Intellectually Handicapped (NZSIH); Royal Commission on Psychopaedic Hospitals; Disabled Persons Community Welfare Act; Westland–Buller branch hosts annual conference, Greymouth

1976   NZ survey, *The Intellectually Handicapped and their Families* published; Margaret Anyon dies

1977   JB Munro succeeds Ray Mathews as general secretary
         Telethon for mental health raises $2 million

1978   International Congress of League in Vienna; annual conference, Nelson

1979   Dr Beasley retires as president; Dr R.T.M. Caseley elected; national office moves to The Terrace, Wellington; Taranaki branch hosts annual conference, New Plymouth

1980   Changes made in composition of NZ Committee; annual conference, Napier

1981   International Year of Disabled Persons; Telethon raises $5 million; IHC policy on education – mainstreaming controversy; annual conference, Blenheim

1982   Annual conference, Wanganui

1983   Disabled Persons' Assembly; People First discussed; annual conference, Canterbury

1984   Third Regional Pacific Conference on Mental Retardation of the International League organised by NZSIH, Wellington

1985   Gumboots for Calves scheme; NZ Institute of Mental Retardation Research Unit in Otago; Sutherland Landskills Programme; People First NZ Inc.; annual conference, Masterton

1986   Self-advocacy gaining ground; annual conference, Timaru

1987   J.G.S. Reid retires as vice-president; Barbara Rocco elected vice-president

1988   Dr Caseley retires as president; Dr Roderick Deane elected new president; Protection of Personal and Property Rights Act; annual conference, Palmerston North

1989   Education Act amendment; national office moves to 15th Floor, Willbank House, 57 Willis St, Wellington; Standards and Monitoring Board established

1990   Human Rights Act; Restructuring of NZSIH; National Special Olympics in Palmerston North; biennial conference, Auckland

1991   Asia and Pacific Action Committee becomes South Pacific Disability Council; Venn Young Report – Review of IHC

1992	Mental Health (Compulsory Assessment and Treatment) Act; biennial conference, Wanganui
1993	People First Conference in Toronto; Keith Anyon dies
1994	Name change to IHC New Zealand Inc.; Dr Roderick Deane retires as president; Barbara Rocco elected president; launch of People First logo at the Beehive; biennial conference, Rotorua
1996	Closure of Templeton and Porirua hospitals announced; biennial conference, Queenstown; Robert Martin elected onto Council, Inclusion International
1997	JB Munro retires as chief executive; Jan Dowland becomes chief executive
1998	IHC Board of Governance established; Don Wills elected president of Inclusion International; Robert Martin third vice-president, Inclusion International; biennial conference, Tauranga
1999	Proposed closure of Kimberley; 50th anniversary celebrations

Intellectual Disabilities:
Support Groups in New Zealand

Genetic Disorder Support Group
Parent to Parent National Office
P O Box 234
Waikato Mail Centre NZ
Tollfree 0508 236 236
Fax (07) 834 1108
Email p2pnation@compuserve.com

Angelman Syndrome Support Group
Angelman Syndrome Family Connections
177 Colombo Road
Masterton
Ph (06) 377 3125

Apert Syndrome Support Group
Apert Network
6 Peter Mulgrew Street
Avondale
Auckland 1007
Ph/Fax (09) 627 9137
Email howrdnan@ihug.co.nz

Autism/Asperger Disorder Support Group
NZ Autistic Association
P O Box 7305
Sydenham
Christchurch
Ph (03) 332 1038
Fax (03) 337 0550
Email m.s.whitworth@xtra.co.nz

Batten Disease Support Group
P O Box 232
Ohakune
Ph (06) 385 8103
Fax (06) 385 8103

Charcot-Marie-Tooth Disease Support Group
CMT International – Representative
P O Box 260
Thames
Ph (07) 868 6375
Fax (07) 868 7677
dentalpd@wave.co.nz

Cornelia de Lange Support Group
11 Winsomere Crescent
Westmere
Auckland
Ph (09) 378 0720

Cranio-Facial Support Group
c/-Apert Network
6 Peter Mulgrew Street
Avondale
Auckland
Ph/Fax (09) 627 9137
Email howrdnan@ihug.co.nz

Down Syndrome Support Group
NZ Down Syndrome Association
P O Box 4142
Auckland
Ph (09) 307 7945
Fax (09) 379 5762
Email garrys@ak.planet.gen.nz
Internet http://www.nzdsa.org.nz/

Fragile X Syndrome Support Group
Fragile X Association of Australia Inc
726 West Coast Road
Waiatarua, Auckland
Ph (09) 814 8828
Email k-vwillie@ihug.co.nz

Klinefelter Syndrome Support Group
New Zealand Klinefelter Association
96 Hair Street
Wainuiomata 6008
Ph (04) 564 4045
Email nzkline@ihug.co.nz
Internet http//homepages.ihug.co.nz/~nzkline

Lysosomal Storage Disease Support Group
1248 High Street
Lower Hutt
Ph (04) 567 5704
Email john@wellink.org.nz
Internet http://www.ldnz.org.nz

New Zealand MPS/ML Family Society
c/- Patricia Zimmerman
1/13 Forest Hill Road
Henderson
Waitakere City
Ph (09) 835 3572
Fax (09) 817 3613

Phenylketonuria Support Group
29a Rangatira Road
Birkenhead

Auckland
Ph (09) 483 7732
Email afrancis@kiwilink.co.nz

Prader-Willi Syndrome Support Group
Prader-Willi Syndrome Association NZ (Inc)
P O Box 143
Masterton
Ph (06) 378 9132
Fax (06) 370 9117
Email pwsanz@xtra.co.nz
Internet http://pwsyndrome.com/NewZealand

Rett Syndrome Support Group
Rett Syndrome Association
P O Box 28-049
Wellington

Trisomy 18,13 Support Group
SOFT (NZ)
Support Organisation for Trisomy 18,13
79 Clawton Street
New Plymouth 4601
Ph (06) 753 2494
Fax (06) 753 5390

Turner Syndrome Support Group
Turner Syndrome Society (NZ) Inc
c/- Parent and Family Resources
P O Box 9407
Newmarket, Auckland
Ph (09) 631 5644
Fax (09) 631 0126
Email heatheralford@hotmail.com

Williams Syndrome Support Group
Louise Smith
NZ Williams Syndrome Association
513 Pages Road
Christchurch 8007
Ph/Fax (03) 382 4100
Email mark.louise@xtra.co.nz

Bibliography

Unpublished

Anyon Papers, IHC library, Wellington.

Botting, R.W.S., Historical Notes on IHC to 1972, IHC library, Wellington.

IHC branch histories, IHC library, Wellington.

Tape-recorded interviews (transcripts held by IHC library, Wellington) with the following: Dr Peter Anyon, Dr Donald Beasley, Stan Botting, J.B. Brotherston, Marion Bruce, Dr R.T.M. Caseley, Jean Clark, Desmond Corrigan, Dr Roderick Deane, Gillian Deane, Robert Martin, JB Munro, Barbara Rocco, G.D. Wills.

Theses

Golding, R.L., 'History of the Auckland Branch of the Intellectually Handicapped Children's Society of New Zealand', University of Auckland, 1967.

Riseborough, A.J., 'The Intellectually Handicapped Children's Society: The First Twenty Years from Protest Group to Welfare Organisation', Victoria University of Wellington, 1986.

Sonntag, E.J., 'Caregiving and Activism: The Experience of Women with Daughters and Sons with Intellectual Disability', University of Waikato, 1993.

Thomson, J.B., 'Indigence to Independence: The Development of Social Policy in New Zealand for People with Learning Disabilities', Massey University, 1995.

Published

Community Moves, vol. 30, No. 1, June 1992–.

Community Moves, August 1993, article on Murphy, Mick.

Community Moves, March 1997, article on Brydone, Tom.

Community Moves, October 1998, article on Brotherston, J.B.

Frame, Janet, *To the Is-land*, Women's Press/Hutchinson Group, 1983.

'Happy 40th Birthday IHC 1949–1989', *The Intellectual Handicap Review*, December 1989.

Intellectual Handicap Review (*IH Review*), official journal of the NZ Society for the Intellectually Handicapped, June–Aug. 1975–June 1991.

Intellectually Handicapped Child, official journal of the Intellectually Handicapped Children's Parents' Association, 1960–75.

Marshall, J.R., *Memoirs, vol. 1, 1912–1960*, Collins, Auckland, 1983.

Mitchell, D.R. and Mitchell, J.W., *Out of the Shadows: A Chronology of Significant Events in the Development of Services for Exceptional Children and Young Persons in New Zealand, 1850–1983*, Dept of Education, Wellington, 1985.

Morrison, A.A., Beasley, D.M.G., and Williamson, K.I., *The Intellectually Handicapped and Their Families: A New Zealand Survey*, Research Foundation of the NZ Society for the Intellectually Handicapped, Wellington, 1976.

Shearer, Ann, *Services to New Zealanders with Intellectual Handicaps*: A Report to the New Zealand Committee of IHC, NZ Society for the Intellectually Handicapped, Wellington, 1984.

Index